MODEL STUDENT ESSAYS

PRENTICE HALL
Upper Saddle River, New Jersey 07458

© 1998 by PRENTICE HALL, INC.
Simon & Schuster / A Viacom Company
Upper Saddle River, New Jersey 07458

ISBN 0-13-645516-6

Printed in the United States of America

Table of Contents

Preface

This collection of essays by students in first-year college writing courses has been compiled from submissions from fifteen different schools across the country. Drawn from over a hundred submissions—from two-year community colleges to four-year universities, from urban campuses to schools in small towns and rural areas, from eighteen-year-old students to students entering college after years out of school—these essays represent a sampling of effective writing as practiced in freshman composition today.

They reflect a wide scope of interests and experiences, as well as an impressive range of writing strategies: careful selection of detail in narration and description; thoughtful use of appropriate examples, comparison and contrast, and causal analysis in developing a subject; clearly organized development in support of a thesis; thorough research and documentation of sources when required; expressive originality when suitable to the topic. They also encompass an interesting variety of voices; each writer has a clear style that in every case well serves his or her purpose in writing. Because discovering one's individual voice is so important for successful writing, we hope that these examples will suggest possibilities that other students can relate to their own writing more directly than they often can examples by professional writers.

In determining the organization for the collection, we were ultimately guided by the submissions themselves. Perhaps not surprisingly, virtually every essay received fell into one of the three categories "Writing to Explore Personal Experience," "Writing to Inform or Explain," or "Writing to Argue a Position." Using these three primary purposes of written communication seemed to provide the most flexible framework for presenting the essays because, within each, a variety of different, more specific writing strategies can be employed: We point out examples of these in the introductions to each chapter. The chapter introductions also provide an opening look at each essay and offer some brief comments about the kinds of writing they represent. Otherwise, we have tried to let the students—and their essays—speak for themselves. (The essays have been edited to conform to standard convention, for matters of clarity, and occasionally for length—just as any writer's work is edited prior to publication. However, such editing has been kept to a minimum; we have not attempted to make the writers here sound more "professional"; these are truly student voices.)

We thank the following instructors for submitting the essays that appear in this collection:

Sharon Gerring, Buffalo State College
Sherill Cobb, Collin County Community College
John Swennsen, De Anza College
Cathryn Amadahl, Harrisonburg Area Community College
S. Bergman, Indiana University—Fort Wayne
Jennifer Annick, Loyola Marymount University
Michael McGeean, Loyola Marymount University
Marie B. Czarnecki, Mohawk Valley Community College
Sandra Petrulionis, Penn State—Altoona
Diane Taylor, Spoon River Community College—Macomb Campus
Barbara Moran, University of San Francisco
Richard Black, Southeast Missouri State University
Michael O'Rourke, Tennessee Technological University
Heidemarie Weidner, Tennessee Technological University
Donnie Yeilding, Central Texas College
Judy Burnham, Tulsa Community College

We would also, of course, like to thank the many students who agreed to submit their papers—not only the ones included here, but all who contributed to such a strong selection of essays to choose from. Making the final choices was often not easy, and many fine essays were edged out only for reasons of space.

If you would like to submit work for a future collection of student writing, you may mail submissions to:

English Editor
Prentice Hall
Humanities and Social Sciences Division
One Lake Street
Upper Saddle River, NJ 07458

A final word about submissions: Each student must include a signed release form for any essays submitted. Essays from several schools could not be considered for this collection because they were not accompanied by an appropriate release. A sample Release Form appears at the end of the book.

We hope students and instructors alike will appreciate working with the variety of student writing that this collection represents. Interesting, accessible, well-written—these are essays to which every student can aspire.

I

Writing To Explore Personal Experience

Each of the student essays in this chapter is based primarily in the writer's personal experience, the purpose being to communicate the effect of those experiences on the writer's life. Some, like Amy Martin and Vincent Lormé, focus on a specific experience of a relatively short duration; others, like Jeana Roberts and Genea Brugh recount a variety of related experiences taking place over the course of time. In some cases the tone is humorous and light-hearted; in others the writers focus more seriously on difficulties they've overcome or problems they have faced. What all the essays have in common is a sense of honesty and thoughtfulness, going beyond simply describing personal experience to suggest the significance of such experience in terms of each writer's individual development and understanding.

The range of these experiences is suitably broad. In "The Greasy Pig" Amy Martin recounts her childhood experience of winning a very unusual contest that led to a new respect from her family. Vincent Lormé recalls his final high school football game, a capstone experience that represents one of his most indelible memories ("What a Long Trip It's Been"). Liz Ortiz, in "The Consequences of Life," writes about making a difficult decision concerning her relationship with a well-loved friend whose drug problems caused her much concern. Jeana N. Roberts explains "How I Fell Through the Cracks and Crawled Back Out Again," looking back as a twenty-nine-year-old returning student on how her earlier educational experiences led her not only to give up on school, but also to decide to pursue an education again. In "Irony" Kimberly Brown offers an impressionistic account of the toll cigarette smoking took on her grandmother—as well as herself. Casey Cummings, in "Employment for Life," also focuses on a beloved grandmother, one she sees as an important role model whose commitment is to be admired. "Reebocks—Don't Fail Me Now," is Genea Brugh's witty account of her experiences as a fairly naive young woman from a rural area when she gets a job with the Postal Department and is assigned to a route in a poor inner-city neighborhood. A former G.I. who served in Saudi Arabia during the Desert Storm conflict, Stanten Adcock describes the intense cold of the desert night and how his experience there led him to chilling revelation ("Lonesome Tumbleweeds"). Finally, in "I Am More" Victoria Mohatt, the daughter of a white father and a black mother, explores the feelings of pain and anger she experiences when friends and acquaintances insist on classifying her as either "black" or "white."

Relying primarily on narration and description, the essays here also suggest the ways that writing about personal experience can incorporate comparing and contrasting ("The Greasy Pig," "Reebocks—Don't Fail Me Now"), cause and effect ("How I Fell Through the Cracks and Crawled Back Out Again," "Lonesome Tumbleweeds"), and even persuasion ("I Am More"). Whatever the strategy, each represents a unique voice exploring the variety of experience that students bring with them to the writing classroom.

The Greasy Pig

Amy Martin
(Monterey, Tennessee)

I don't know where or when it was that I first learned of the gender gap, but I believe it was around the time that I was about six years old. My brothers played baseball when I was young, and I yearned to be out there on the field too. But to my dismay, the only position that I was allowed to hold was that of the water girl. My Aunt Georgie lived across the street from the baseball field and I can remember running back and forth from the field to her house carrying an empty six-pack of coke bottles and filling them with water as fast as the boys' team could empty them again. This must have been one of my earliest memories of how girls and boys were not created equal.

Later in my early life, I remember my mother calling, "Hurry up, Amy, and get your shoes on, we're all going down to the ball field." It was Independence Day. The year was 1971, and I was ten years old and very much a tomboy, due to the fact that I have six older brothers. The entire town was about to begin celebrating the Fourth of July. I could just smell the scent of the hot dogs and hamburgers coming from the concession stand. I jumped into our hideous station wagon—Moby Dick, as I liked to refer to it—and off we went.

We parked the car at Aunt Georgie's house. Dad and Mom visited with Aunt Georgie while my brothers and I ran on across the street to join the crowd that had gathered. Everyone in town was there, young and old. It was late afternoon, but the sun was still pretty high in the sky and the summer sun felt so good. Music played, and there was lots of laughter as everyone was having a good time. Jeff, Luke, and I headed toward the bleachers. One of the men in charge was announcing the beginning of the water balloon contest. My brothers ran off to join in as I watched. Oh, how I wished that I had the courage to go and join in, but my Mother had asked me not to get my dress dirty. How I hated being a girl sometimes. Just look at the boys, uninhibited and running wild and free. Boys were just allowed to do so much more than girls. I watched from the stands, and I was so proud when Luke came in second place. They gave him an all-day pass to the community swimming pool. Wow. Dad wouldn't let me go swimming at the pool. I had asked him over and over to let me go with the boys for a swim, but he was so overly protective. He'd take me swimming out at the creek, but I wasn't allowed to go down by the park to the community pool. He didn't want me "naked," as he called it, in public. I wasn't sure if he thought I'd drown or if I would just grow up on him.

"That's it," I thought. "Mom and Dad are still at Aunt Georgie's, so I'll just join in some of the festivities while they're out of sight and maybe I can win a pass to the pool. If I can win a few all-day passes, surely there's no way Dad will refuse to let me go."

I ran out onto the infield as quickly as I could and just in time to join in the wheelbarrow race. My best friend, Debbie, was there, so I grabbed her by the arm and pulled her into the starting line with me. The whistle blew and off we raced. We were hilarious. Debbie was trying to hold my legs up, but I was moving so fast down the field that she dropped me twice. Who would have thought that in the end we would come in third place? We won hamburgers and French fries at the concession stand. Shucks. Of course, I was pleased, but food was not what I was after. I was determined and didn't care if it hair-lipped the devil, I'd win tickets to the pool or bust.

The next contest was to see who could hit a softball the furthest. I elected to sit this one out. Debbie and I went to the concession stand to cash in our vouchers.

"Debbie, I've just got to win tickets to the swimming pool today. You know that's the only way that Dad and Mom are going to let me go," I explained.

"Do you really think they'll let you go to the pool if you win the tickets?" she asked.

"Surely to goodness they'd just have to let me go if I win them, and you've got to help me. We're gonna enter every contest they have for the rest of the night, even the Greasy Pig Contest," I declared.

Everyone in town was waiting for the famous Greasy Pig Contest. When five o'clock finally rolled around, I was grateful that Mom and Dad were still across the street. There must have been a couple hundred of us on that field. Oh, what fun. Two men had the poor little pig as best they could, but there must have been an inch or more of grease on that animal, making it difficult for them to hang on. The pig slipped from their hands and off it went inside the fence. And then, off we went too. I imagine that we looked like a swarm of bees just flying all over the field trying to catch that pig. I saw a girl in the next grade up from me grab the pig, but she didn't get a good hold on

3

it. "There's still a chance," I thought. Then a boy a few years older than me tackled the poor little thing, but it wiggled loose. That's when I came flying through the air. I grabbed with all my might and latched onto the pig's rear right leg. My thumb and forefinger were holding on to its ankle so tightly that I squeezed the grease off in the process and got a good hold.

"I got it!" I screamed, "I got it. I got it, I caught the greasy pig!" A few of the kids tried to lay claim to catching it, but the crowd pointed at me. I caught the greasy pig!

By that time my parents had come over to see what the commotion was about. "Where's Amy?" my Dad asked the boys.

"She's been out there in the ball ground chasing that pig, and what's better, she caught it!" Jeff reported. I was told later that evening that my Dad just grinned.

Catching that pig was about the proudest moment of my young life, and my parents were proud of me too—as well as my superior brothers. The two men in charge led me to the pitcher's mound along with my pig, which I was still holding onto. The rest of the kids followed. My Dad, Mom, and brothers proudly joined me on the mound. "She's a real scrapper," I heard my Dad say.

"And now, the grand prize goes to Amy Laura Callahan for catching the greasy pig—free passes to the community swimming pool for the rest of the summer!" said the announcer.

""Yippee! Oh, Dad, can I please go swimming this summer, please?" I pleaded.

My Dad looked proudly at me. "If you can catch a greasy pig, then I guess you are big enough to take care of yourself. Sure, you can go swimming with the boys from now on."

That day I sort of earned my independence and tightened the gender gap a bit. I even began playing softball. No longer was there anything that I could not "tackle," no pun intended. I took my winnings home—my pig and my independence.

-Tennessee Technical University
Michael O'Rourke, Instructor

What a Long Trip It's Been

Vincent Lormé
(East Concord, New York)

Football is a game of power, pride, and concentration, a game in which your heart and your pride must overpower your fears. I played Little

League and high school football from the age of nine. From the beginning of my Little League career to my last game, I always loved playing. Football consumed me.

The final game of what seemed to be my endless career took place at Rich Stadium in Orchard Park, New York—home of the Buffalo Bills, the second best team in the world. The Section VI High School Football Championship was held there on November 3, 1996.

As I snapped my shoulderpad clips into place, my mind and heart were at a standstill—only twenty-five minutes before the biggest game of my life. As we slowly finished suiting up, our coach ran through the game plan to make sure we were all on the same page. The final five minutes were silent. Sitting in Andre Reed's locker (a leading receiver for the Buffalo Bills), I could feel the sweat starting to bead on my forehead and my heart pumping out of my chest. Then the words came from Coach Duprey: "This is it. Everything you have worked for comes down to this game. If you want it, then go get it." Nothing more needed to be said.

We anxiously filed into the stadium's tunnel and arranged ourselves into a single-file line led by the captains. A chilly November breeze flowed through the dark tunnel, at the end of which I could see the stadium's bright lights. Slowly, we made our way toward the entrance. With every step closer I began to reflect on my past—the steps, the struggles, and the perseverance it took to reach the championship. Getting to where I was represented a victory in itself, but winning would be the ultimate accomplishment.

Little League started everything off for me. I was a ten-year-old boy doing what I loved to do. At the time, my biggest challenge was to get down to the 120 pound weight limit. I spent most practices running around the track carrying a couple of garbage bags to try to sweat the weight off. Even though I didn't make weight for most of the games, I loved practicing with the rest of my friends. This continued for the next few years.

Every week, my Little League friends and I would go to the varsity football games. As we stood in jerseys that fell past our knees, we would fantasize on how great it would be to play varsity. I remember saying many times, "I'm going to be like him when I grow up," pointing to one of the players on the field. From that moment on, I was dedicated to being the best football player I could be. During the eighth grade, I decided to transfer to high school football and play for the Springville Griffins a year early.

It was the hardest thing I had ever done, but the next day I came back for more. High school seemed to go by quickly, along with the football seasons. My team had some rough times, so our senior season was going to make or break our record. Determined to win, we found out we were unstoppable. Week after week we defeated teams by anywhere from twenty to sixty points.

We finished out the regular season with eight wins and zero losses. We were named the Section VI, Division IV champions. (The section is the area of New York you are in, and the division is the size of your school.)

Our team traveled to Albion, New York, for the play-off game. At the end of the first half of play, we were losing by three points, but it wasn't over yet. We came out in the second half and scored two unanswered touchdowns. The win sent us to play at Rich Stadium the following week. Excited wasn't the word for how we all felt. We did it! We made it! We were going to Rich Stadium!

I can still hear the sound of our hometown fans cheering as we began to file out of the tunnel and into Rich Stadium. The lights were bright, and the ground felt like a tightly woven carpet. We slowly jogged along the sidelines while clapping in a steady rhythm. We lined up in front of the captains and began stretching. Counting out loud with the captains—"one-one thousand, two-one thousand, three-one thousand"—I looked around and thought about how large the stadium was. Even though there weren't 80,000 screaming fans, it still felt good to be there. I thought about how glad I was that I put on an extra T-shirt because there were strong winds blowing along the stadium's floor. "Eight-one thousand, nine-one thousand...." Between the stretching, we all worked together to get motivated by punching each other in the chest or screaming loudly.

At this time, our opponents entered the stadium floor. They were the Olean Huskies—our rival, our enemy, our obstacle; we must beat them. The sounds of both teams warming up, trying to intimidate one another, and the fans' cheering echoed throughout the stadium walls and beyond.

The time on the pre-game clock slowly ticked down: 31, 30, 29.... Both teams lined up on the sidelines and awaited the start of the game: 3, 2, 1. The referees took the field, and an announcer said, "Please stand for our National Anthem." I pried off my helmet, setting it by my side and placed my hand across my chest covering my heart. Though I have heard that anthem every game I have played, for some reason it had a much greater meaning on this day. It made me realize that, win or lose, we had all come a long way together. We had watched each other grow, as teammates and as friends, over the years.

At the completion of the anthem, the fans went wild, and the players took the field for the opening kickoff. As soon as the referee had blown the whistle, Olean kicked the ball into the Griffins' territory. We muscled the ball up to the thirty-seven yard line. Our offensive team, which is the team used to score, formed a huddle until a play was called. After that, we clapped hands and said "break" at the same time as we moved to the line of scrimmage. The first contact of the game would determine which team was stronger, so it was important to hit hard and not be hit. I stepped to the line and waited anxiously for the quarterback's call while placing my elbows on my knees. On "down," I placed my right fist on the ground, and my eyes looked up at my opponent through the bars of my face mask. The quarterback continued: "Set, hut-one, hut-two." On "hut-two," I plunged off the line and connected head-to-head, shoulder-to-shoulder with my opponent across the line. It was a power struggle. If I hit him hard enough he might fear being hit for the rest of the game. In fact, the first hit was very equal; we both hit hard and were looking forward to the next. With two excellent teams on the field, it's hard to overpower the other. You basically have to wait for the other team to make a mistake. As the game went on, both teams struggled for the first score. We were the best football teams in the league, so scoring against either side would not be easy. At the end of the first half of play, it remained a scoreless game. Each team was trying to outsmart the other, but doing it unsuccessfully.

As I jogged off the field towards the locker room for the half-time break, I had time to collect my thoughts and concentrate on the second half. It was still anyone's ball game, and I knew the second half would be the hardest of the season. I glanced over at the fans only to see hundreds of people clapping and cheering, yet I was unable to hear them. The stadium was in a comfortable silence. It wasn't until I pushed open that heavy cold, steel locker-room door with the Buffalo Bills insignia in the center that I could hear once again. I unstrapped my shoulderpads so that I could breathe a little more easily and sat down in silence while Coach Duprey discussed the game plan for the second half. After he was done, a few of the other players and I discussed what we needed to do in the second half in order to come out with the win.

"Get suited up, it is time to play some football," Coach Duprey said.

My elbows were sore and beginning to swell up, so I slid on my elbow guards and strapped my shoulderpads back into place. We filed into the tunnel and lined ourselves up for our entrance back into the stadium. I led the team to the north end of the field and circled around for warm-ups. At the sound of the whistle, we stood on the sidelines awaiting the start of the second half. It was like the beginning of the game all over again.

We kicked the ball off and Olean brought it up to the forty-two yard line. The level of emotion on the field was immeasurable. We had to stay together as a team if we wanted to win. They moved the ball slowly but nevertheless effectively towards the goal line. There was no time to get worried. We had to stay focused. With a few good plays, they muscled the ball into the endzone for the first score of the game. After missing the extra point, Olean led six to zero. Now with the ball in our hands we tried to do the same. It wasn't until the end of the third quarter that we found a series of plays that worked for us. With those plays we scored our first touchdown of the game.

After kicking the extra point, we took the lead by a score of seven to six.

With Olean controlling the ball, their quarterback threw a long pass which ended up hitting one of our linebackers on his helmet, sending the ball up in the air. Our best cornerback came down with the interception. With just a few more plays we scored our second touchdown but missed the extra point. We were leading by a score of thirteen to six. With six minutes and forty-three seconds left in the game, Olean completed a sixty-two yard pass-and-run play, which left them on our twelve-yard line. We had to stop them.

As I stood on the line of scrimmage, my only thought was to get the quarterback. The ball was snapped, and I took my steps across the line of scrimmage. The quarterback rolled to my side and I began rushing towards him. I stepped up and hit him as hard as I could across the waist. As he fell, he tossed the ball to a running back behind him who somehow found his way into the endzone. After running the extra point in, Olean led the game fourteen to thirteen.

Olean then stopped us in the next series of plays and with a little over two minutes left in the game, they once again took control of the ball. We were able to stop Olean and force them to punt from their twenty-eight yard line. We blocked the kick and recovered the fumble. We had excellent field position to score and a chance to win the game. In three plays we moved the ball to the eight-yard line. Because there was little time and no more time-outs left, we decided to kick a field goal for the win. With just twelve seconds left, we knew we were going to win or lose on this last play.

As we broke out of the huddle for the last time as a team, we held hands up to the line of scrimmage. I placed my hands on the ground in front of me and watched a bead of sweat roll off my nose and land on the field between my feet. The stadium was silent to me, as it had been for most of the game. The snap was gone, and the lineman made an unbreakable wall in front of the ball. I heard the ball holder yell "fire," which meant that something went wrong in the backfield and he was going to try to run to my right. The runner tried to make it into the endzone but was tackled just inches of that line separating a win from a loss. The final score of the game was fourteen to thirteen, and the champions were the Olean Huskies.

Immediately, a feeling of sadness and disappointment rushed through my body. I looked at the cheering fans, my teammates, and my opponents, but I was still unable to hear any of them. I stood in silence, looking and thinking of how far we have come over the years and how much I appreciated playing with my teammates. It was sad to think that this would be the last time I suited up, played, and struggled with those guys that I knew so well. As a coach long ago once told me, "No regrets. If you gave everything you had to give, you should have no regrets." After that game I had no regrets. I had just finished playing the best and most memorable game of my career.

After shaking hands with the other team and talking to the fans and the news crews, I made my way toward the tunnel of Rich Stadium for the last time.

As I was walking up the tunnel, I stopped and turned around for one last look, one last moment before leaving. About ten feet from me stood two little boys with jerseys on that fell past their knees. The one boy picked up his hand and pointed at me saying, "I'm going to be like you when I grow up." I smiled at him and proceeded up that long, cold, dark tunnel to the locker room.

-Buffalo State College
Sharon Gerring, Instructor

The Consequences of Life
Liz Ortiz
(Paterson, New Jersey)

How can you help someone with a drug problem when the person doesn't realize he or she has a problem? During my lifetime I've come across drug users and drug sellers. I've heard all the stories and felt great compassion and sorrow for them all. Each of them had a reason for taking the path he or she chose, reasons ranging from being sexually abused to having to sell drugs in order to have food on the table and clothes to wear. At one point or another, though, they were all able to find the strength to change and live a more productive life. I never gave up on them or thought less of them. I knew that being a true friend meant "sticking around" and waiting for each of them to reach out the other fifty percent so I could help them out.

My "sticking around" though changed when I met Prasand. He was different from all the rest; he actually had two loving parents, lived in a great neighborhood, and had, in my eyes, a lot of advantages. Prasand also become very special to me; I shared things with him I never told anyone else. We bonded, and he became one of my closest friends. That's why when I had to let him go, it became one of the hardest things I've ever done so far. I loved him so dearly, but he was tearing a piece of my heart out every time he headed closer towards self-destruction.

Prasand first saw me at a show I was performing in and asked a cast member to introduce us. When I first saw him, the thing I noticed were his eyes. They weren't green, blue, or hazel but stood out just as beautifully. His eyes were dark and mysterious, and I could see my reflection in them so clearly. As I looked deeper into his eyes, in a sense I saw past my reflection and

9

straight into his heart. They say that the eyes are the windows of the soul; all I know is that I saw someone full of love, warmth, kindness, and great innocence, with a wonderful story to tell. I don't believe in love at first sight, but whatever this feeling was, it was strong and I felt an immediate bond with him. Besides capturing me with his eyes, he was very good-looking otherwise. Prasand had jet black hair, a great body, lips that any girl would love to kiss, and a smile that could capture anyone's heart. We didn't get a chance to talk long, but we did exchange telephone numbers. As soon as I had his number in my hands, I knew I was definitely going to "dial those digits."

I called Prasand two days later, and we hit it off right from the start. At first we would talk about twice a week, but as we started feeling more comfortable with each other, the phone calls increased. It was difficult to see each other because we lived in different towns, so we made sure to fill each other in on what was going on in our lives.

As the months flew by, our friendship grew and so did my feelings for him. He had become my best friend, and I found myself slowly falling in love with him. How could I resist? He seemed like the perfect boyfriend. Whenever I had a bad day, he was there to listen and comfort me, as I was there for him. We shared our joys as well as our sorrow with each other. He would even write and mail me letters, which I thought was very sweet and showed he thought of me often.

Even though we were great friends, Prasand and I had a lot of differences. First, although we are both Hispanic, we are from different cultures. I'm Puerto Rican and Prasand is Colombian. Moreover, Prasand doesn't speak a word of Spanish and knows very little about Colombian culture because he and his little brother were adopted by a Jewish couple and brought to the United States from Columbia when he was very young.

We also differed in terms of the kind of people we chose to be our friends and in the fact that he would smoke marijuana and sell it as well. Prasand's so-called friends were heavily into drugs like acid, cocaine, and even heroin. My friends, on the other hand, wouldn't even go near the kind of drugs they tried. At first, Prasand said he wasn't into marijuana that much, but as time passed by, he used it even more. Before I knew it, he was even experimenting with cocaine. When he described to me how he tried it at a friend's party, I was in complete shock and reminded him how he used to say he would never try that kind of drug. We spent so many countless days and nights talking about his involvement in drugs and when he was going to stop. In fact, every time I went to his house, that was the first thing we would talk about. Eventually, we came to the agreement that he would stop his involvement with drugs once the new school year started.

Once the new school year came around however, Prasand went back on our agreement. The situation became even worse; every weekend when he went "clubbing," he was getting high. He used drugs like ecstasy and acid; he even mixed these drugs with alcohol. These irresponsible actions had him hospitalized twice. My words of guidance at this point had run out. He thought that what he was doing was "just fine," but I knew he was heading down the path of self-destruction. I couldn't help him because he felt as though he didn't need a change in his life. I was spending endless nights worrying about his safety, wondering to myself, "Is he going to make it home tonight or not?" At this point, I also had my own share of hardships and couldn't handle both of our problems. Then the hard part came: how do I let go of someone who means so much to me but is out of my reach? He was not only destroying his life, but he was dragging mine down as well. I realized I had no choice; I had to do what I had to do. So, finally, the time came, and even though it may sound cruel and wrong, I let him go.

Now a day cannot pass by without him coming into my thoughts. I'm haunted by the feeling that I did the wrong thing by letting him go. I still don't know whether I was right or wrong in doing so. I'm just too scared to confront him. I don't know how he would react in person. Even worse, I don't know how I would react if I had to go visit him in a graveyard. If he's dead, I know it will destroy part of me. Maybe one day, though, I will find a force within myself to go out and find him. I just hope and pray I'm not disappointed and that he is alive and doing "just fine."

-William Patterson College
Carol Gabel, Instructor

How I Fell Through The Cracks And Crawled Out Again

Jeana N. Roberts
(Steelton, Pennsylvania)

Have you ever had the experience of equating your life to clichés? I find myself doing it quite often. I may hear a phrase or nursery rhyme, and then "Bingo!," the next thing I know I am spiraled back in time to the incident that phrase recalls. One day, I would love to write a story full of clichés and unmercifully drive some poor English teacher to the brink of insanity. But, alas, my fanciful thoughts of mischievous acts will have to wait as I endeavor to compose a very serious essay entitled, "Why I Am In College."

I started my education in Catholic school, where I was taught how to learn It's difficult to explain what I mean, but it's not so much what subject materials I was taught as how I was taught to learn them. I knew I was receiving a good education—even at the age of nine. When I was in second grade, I was sent to the third grade class for phonics, and I remember performing math calculations accurately and swiftly, as the teacher wrote on the chalkboard. I really enjoyed school then.

Along with fourth grade came the first of many changes in my life—public education. My new school brought with it new faces (and some old ones from the projects), new teachers (male and female teachers—both wearing pants!), basketball courts, a baseball field, and a bigger playground. I still was sent to a different class for English, and now for math, too. The kids in my class never teased me about it, so I thought it was cool not to sit in the same classroom all day. I entered spelling bees and literature contests; I joined the chorus; I participated in talent shows; and I auditioned for parts in plays even though I was shy. I truly looked forward to school on Mondays. If I stayed in that school district for the seventh grade, I would have begun accelerated classes. But all good things must come to and end. Why? Probably so we don't stop appreciating them.

"Step on a crack break you mother's back...." I wonder what happens to your mother's back if you fall in a crack, as I did. Seventh grade. New school. New school district. Lost records? Assigned to general studies! Uh-oh. Sinking fast.

Life.
What a
whirl
wind.

That was the last time for a long time school concerned me. "When in Rome...." I guess I tried at first. I did my homework. I did my classmates' homework. I took my tests, and somehow my completed test always found its way to the corner of my desk at the request of neighboring peers who just wanted to check and see if their answers were correct.

In eighth grade someone figured out a "boo-boo" had been made, and now my guidance counselor wanted to make things up to me. Nope. I enjoyed not spending a lot of time doing homework or studying for tests. I already knew everything the general studies students were doing. This was a breeze. Since I didn't have to spend time studying, I had a lot of extra time on my hands. "Idle minds are the devil's playground." That's the truth. So for the next three years, I dibbled in this and dabbled in that. Nothing or no one kept my attention for very long. Until the eleventh grade.

Accounting I—or was it Bookkeeping? It doesn't matter what you call it—a rose by any other name would still smell so sweet. To me, accounting was that rose. I breathed it, I lived it. For the first time since the sixth grade, I had found something that intrigued me, enticed me to study even. Idle mind no more. I had found my niche. Numbers. Debits and credits. Assets and liabilities. Capital. Oh, the formulas. The principles—the G.A.A.P.s. I could see the sun shining brilliantly into the crevice where I had lain for so long.

I studied faithfully. For the first time since entering that school district, I didn't have time for friends or foolishness. Just say "No." I had work to do. Why weren't they at home doing their homework? I began studying moments after arriving home from school. I broke for dinner and occasionally I would watch a favorite TV show. At night, the thick, hard-bound pages of my accounting textbook became my pillow. In the morning, I would lift my head and smooth the wrinkles from my bible. My salvation. I must have died and gone to Heaven.

I took with me to twelfth grade a new attitude, but also, unfortunately, a new class schedule. Accounting II required two class periods. That, plus the other required courses, left no spare time for study halls. How could this be? I couldn't get through the entire school year without study halls. When would I do my homework (other than accounting)? I may not have earned the best (or even next to best) grades these past five years, but I always did enough to pass. How could I make it though my senior year?

I brushed the moisture from my lashes as I hurriedly turned from the accounting teacher with my signed withdrawal slip in my hand. "A mind is a terrible thing to waste." I now had two study halls, back-to-back, every school day. Out of the six-and-one-half hours I was required to be in school, two hours would be free to do my homework. What did I do at home? The same things I did from seventh through tenth grades—a little of this and a little of that. Of course, I passed—just barely. I didn't shed one tear at graduation. It amazed me the people who were crying. All I wanted to do since coming here was leave—save the eleventh grade—and I was exuberant! All's well that ends well. The only problem was: I still had to get through this thing called "life."

"Time sure flies when you're having fun." Over the next ten years I tried many things: college (dropped out during the first semester), travel school (learned how to purchase an airline ticket for the many trips I took to relieve the boredom of life), several jobs (if twenty-five can be considered "several"): check processor, bartender, receptionist, cab driver, dispatcher, disgruntled postal employee, data entry operator, inventory clerk, claims examiner—the list really does go on and on. The only things I truly enjoyed were working with numbers and traveling. Two plus two equals four and what I was adding up was: If I went back to school for something I liked to do—accounting—I could earn enough money to travel as often as I wanted. Okay, so I don't have the "I want to save the world" motive. I just want to live a happy and fulfilling life.

So here I am. Back in school and loving every minute of it. I even enjoy all of my classes. How? I just view them as rungs on my ladder of success. I can't turn back the hands of time, but if I had stopped and listened to the meanings of some of those overused and outdated words and phrases, I may have been saved a lifetime (twenty-nine years) of experience. Well, you live and you learn.

-Harrisonburg Area Community College
Cathryn Amdahl, Instructor

Irony
Kimberly Brown
(Utica, New York)

I am a small child gazing at the wondrous white powder circling me. I can feel each snowflake melting the moment it touches my cheeks. My backyard haven looks beautiful covered in shimmering flecks of light and color. A snowman stands at attention near the trees my grandfather planted last spring. Just saplings, they're not much taller than the snowman. I hear the window sliding up, and I can see her warm smile and twinkling eyes watching me as she exhales a blue puff of smoke from in between her lips. The cigarette done, she flicks it into a snowbank.

Yesterday was the last day of second grade. I can smell the familiar comforting scents of fresh apples and cinnamon drifting out the window into the bright sunshine below. The aroma is stabbing at my senses, making my mouth water. The heat from the sun warming my face, I slowly swim back and forth in my modest pool. Hearing the windows slide, I look up and there she is. She looks tired, as if she had a long hard day at work. She finishes her after lunch smoke with a sigh and a flick. I can see the still burning butt not far from me, blueish-grey smoke filtering up through the green blades of grass.

It's autumn now, with the leaves in full color. The apprehension of entering junior high has subsided, and I am sitting under the now mature saplings, struggling with my homework. The backyard seems smaller, now that I've grown up some. I feel a light breeze pushing cool air and leaves all around me. I hear the lock click, and the tired sound of the window sliding up. I see her ashen face looking down at me. It must be the twilight; her eyes seem dark and far away. As she flicks her butt into the backyard, she exhales a carbon monoxide-filled plume of smoke. She looks at me and smiles, but it

14

almost seems as if she is looking through me. I wave as she turns to go.

Sitting in my backyard, looking in the direction of my school, I see hundreds of balloons let free in celebration of National Smoke Out Day. I should be there celebrating also, but instead I feel cold and numb. I cannot get her image out of my mind. I should picture her in the window, smiling as always, eyes twinkling. Instead, I envision her face, looking though the window-like opening of the coffin. Her eyes and lips are glued shut, and she is wearing orange pancake makeup in an attempt to cover her mottled skin. It is an image that will haunt me for years to come.

As I watched the last few balloons floating up to heaven, I take one more drag off my cigarette, exhale blue smoke from in between my lips, and flick my cigarette into the green grass.

-Mohawk Valley Community College
Marie B. Czarnecki, Instructor

Employment For Life
Casey Cummings
(Lampasas, Texas)

At five-thirty every morning, she begins her day. In a sleepy haze, she awakens and stumbles through the misty grayness of the morning to the coffee pot. As she begins the brew, she will read a little of her Bible, and collect her thoughts for the day. When the coffee is finished, she cooks and serves breakfast to her husband of forty-nine years. Next, she does housework such as ironing and dishes. Soon it is time for her to get dressed and head to work, as her husband does the same. At the age of sixty-eight, my grandmother strives very hard and has more dedication than anybody I know. She has taught me through her example that if you want something out of life, you have to put something in.

Even as a very small child, my grandmother worked hard. She grew up on a family farm with more than enough brothers and sisters, and not enough food or living space. The family had to work hard to stay ahead. My grandmother began to pick cotton with her brothers and sisters when she was barely six. Long days in the burning hot fields of the Texas panhandle picking cotton are hard on a young girl. But my grandma wanted to make her papa proud. So she worked. She worked hard. Sometimes, she would have to stop and wrap up her bleeding fingers, only to turn around and start picking again.

When my grandma turned eighteen, she met my grandfather, and her days of picking cotton ended. After they had been married for two years, they

15

had the first of their three children. The oldest child was only eight years older than the youngest. Every weekend grandma would load up her three children and head to the laundromat. When her two boys were one and three years old, they were both in diapers at the same time. Grandma said that this is when she got to know the laundromat attendant very well! My grandmother raised her children and held a full-time job at the same time. As well as all that, she enjoyed doing volunteer work in her community. Sometimes with all these responsibilities, grandma would have to get up as early as four o'clock in the morning to do the housework before the children were up. For the next twenty years of her life, my grandmother cooked, cleaned, worked, and raised a family.

In addition to being a very hard worker, my grandmother is also very dedicated. Her greatest dedication is to the Lord, and she prays for her family every day. With all she has to do, she finds time every day to read her Bible. I have many memories of her sharing this with me when I would sleep over. Grandma tries hard not to miss a Sunday at church. She says "A Sunday without church is like a summer without sunshine." She is dedicated to her church community. She teaches Sunday School and helps in the church office. If anything ever needs to be done, the church community comes to her. One time, in the middle of the summer, she helped to rebuild an old tabernacle that had fallen victim to the harsh Texas weather. My grandma takes care of the people of her church. When people are sick, they know they can rely on her to help them out. If they can't drive, or don't have a car, she will always give them a ride.

My grandmother is also very dedicated to her family. She has five grandchildren and one great-granddaughter. She loves children! Once I asked my grandma why she still had to work. She smiled and said, "I like to work." I know the reason she works is in order to have extra money to buy her grandchildren presents at Christmas time. I remember one Christmas she drove eighty miles to buy my cousin something she thought he would like. No matter what the occasion, there will be presents that she worked hard to buy.

If most people had been working hard at one thing for over sixty years, they would be ready to stop and take a rest. My grandmother won't do that. She has been working hard at and is dedicated to life. She has taught me that if you want a happy life, you have to work hard, and make yours that way. My grandma always says, "What doesn't kill us will only make us stronger."

-Central Texas College
Donnie Yeilding, Instructor

Reebocks—Don't Fail Me Now

Genea Brugh
(Fort Wayne, Indiana)

I had everything a kid could want, and more. We lived one field away from six hundred acres of forest preserve. My playground consisted of the Isaac Walton League and the Sarah McMillen Girl Scout Camp.

The steep ravines made for the greatest downhill foot races you can imagine. As long as we picked up our feet to avoid protruding tree roots and underbrush, we stayed upright. Large rocks were rare, so even a nose dive wouldn't have killed us. The huge old oak and maple trees growing out of the sides of the ravines had perfect limbs for tying a rope to so we could swing to the other side like Tarzan.

Hunting was not allowed, so we didn't have to worry about men with guns mistaking us for deer. The only people we ever ran into back there were terrified Girl Scouts from the city worrying about spiders in their hair and the occasional canoeist on Cedar Creek.

By the time I was eighteen years old, the only dangers I had encountered were broken bones, frostbite, blue racers, wasps, and corn spiders that looked frighteningly similar to black widows to me. I didn't even know "bad guys" existed.

Two years later I saw an ad in the paper announcing that the Post Office was hiring. I thought, "I'd be a great mailman. I've spent my whole life hiking through hazardous terrain. Plus, I hear the pay is good." So off I marched to take the postal test. I aced it and started delivering mail at the ripe old age of twenty-one. Little did I know what I had gotten myself into.

I had never even driven though a high crime area, let alone walked around all day in one. I was thankful I didn't understand the words that were being hollered out of car windows and off front porches at me. I had the distinct feeling there were references to certain anatomical parts, though.

In a matter of weeks I learned the difference between what I saw and didn't see. For example, the guns, small baggies, and money changing hands were invisible. I did report the domestic violence, however. I was armed only with my Reebocks and a can of pepper spray. The group of guys behind the liquor store on the corner of Lewis and Hanna had .38s, .44s, .45s, and .357s. No contest!

After those first scary months, I notices a difference in what the guys on the porches and corners would say. The suggestive comments filled with four-letter words gradually became, "Hey Mail Lady, how's it going? Want me to carry your bag for you?" The comments were almost friendly. If a new guy was with the "corner regulars" and started harassing me, the regulars guy was with the "corner regulars" and started harassing me, the regulars would stick up for me, telling him to leave me alone "'cause she's all right."

After that I felt a lot safer. I still had to verbally call the occasional bluff, but for the most part, if I spoke decently—and for some reason speaking loudly was better—I was treated decently. Except for a few isolated incidents, as long as I was friendly and kept walking at the same pace, I was left alone.

A few new situations I encountered delivering mail were not so easily overcome. I had heard of strip joints, but had certainly never been inside one. Over the years I have finally come to the conclusion that the men hanging out in these places, who feel it necessary to harass the mail lady when she makes a delivery, cannot be placated. They are mean and nasty no matter what I do. That's when it's time to call their bluff and stick up for myself. Sometimes my language is as colorful as theirs, but at least it shuts them up. Thank God the bouncers are always at the front door in these places. If the troublemaker decides to follow me out, the bouncer delays him at least enough so I get a head start. Reeboks—don't fail me now! If I never see the inside of Poor John's or the Boom Boom Saloon again, it'll be fine with me!

I used to believe that most people were good. The playground bullies at school were the only exception I knew. As I encountered more and more downright mean-spirited people, I began to seriously question that belief. What kind of people don't bother to clear the snow and ice off their uneven porch steps and have the gall to say, "You're late!"? What are people thinking when they hand me a package and ask, "How much postage does this need?," and then get rude when I don't have a postage scale in my mailbag to weigh it?

The absolute meanest things I hear are right after an unrestrained dog tries to—or succeeds in—biting me. The owner is indignant with me because I'm trying to defend myself against his dog. "He's trying to bite you because you're trying to mace him." Oh please! These dog owners don't think I need all my fingers or both my legs and arms?

Not all of my experiences in this job have had a negative effect on me. Some of the things I've seen have taught me invaluable lessons about respect, sympathy, and patience. I've met the sweetest and hardest-working people you can imagine. I've seen people go out of their way to make my job easier. The little old ladies who stand behind their screen doors with hot chocolate for me in January are the same ladies waiting with ice cold lemonade in August.

I've seen seventy-five-year-old men with bad hearts and bad backs trying to get the snow shoveled off the sidewalk before I get there. Mr. Carpenter even shovels a path through the drifts across the yard, so I don't have to walk clear down to the sidewalk and back up again. These insights into

When I see a grandmother get tears in her eyes because I've delivered a letter that isn't even close to being correctly addressed from her six-year-old grandson, I feel richer. When Mrs. McKeeman makes me come in to meet her children and grandchildren when they're visiting, I feel honored. When Mrs. Schilling starts crying when I ring her doorbell to hand her the mail because she'll fall if she steps out onto the ice, I'm rewarded just by seeing her gratitude.

I see the mean, ugly side of life and how it affects people, but I also get to see that there are still wonderful, warm-hearted people living right next door to them. It doesn't matter what town you live in, you can always find people who enrich your life simply by who they are.

I was innocent and naive when I started delivering mail. What I've experienced has caused me to be a bit more skeptical about human nature and people's intentions, and it may have produced some unsightly calluses in my attitude, but I wouldn't trade the knowledge I've gained for anything.

-Indiana University-Purdue University, Fort Wayne
S. Bergman, Instructor

Lonesome Tumbleweeds
Stanten A. Adcock
(Table Grove, Illinois)

The wind howled across the desert like a freight train highballing down a railtrack in Kansas. As it rolled along, it sucked up particles of sand to hurl against the unprotected surfaces of my skin. Mercilessly, it pounded my body and tore at the all too flimsy poncho I was wearing. A steady rhythm of cracks and snaps rose above the roar of the wind as if to mock my feeble attempt at protection from the wind and cold. Tiny specks of sand pelted my face and neck and sandblasted free the dirt accumulated from three days without a shower. My thoughts roamed to days not long before when a warm shower was more than a memory and made me thankful for the force of the wind blowing my own stench out into the empty desert plain. I could only guess as to "Old Sheik Wind's" evil intentions because he was an invisible enemy. As it was, everything out here was unseen.

The desert night was almost over but the darkness would remain for at least another hour. The darkness was always the worst part. It surrounded us so wholly and completely that it left an empty feeling like a huge icicle deep within our hearts: blackness so harsh that nothing can be seen and yet everything imagined. Even blind people have walls and obstacles to impede their progress and at the same time help them navigate, but out here there is only the harsh, bitter wind and its purpose is to hurt and maim, not one of mercy. The darkness envelops us and draws us into its angry grasp, refusing to let any friendly light enter this empty hole of despair. It is almost impossible to believe my eyes are open except for the bitterly cold wind pushing tears across my cheeks as I strain to see something, anything.

The cold is as unforgiving as the hangman's noose. At first it merely tastes the skin where it is unprotected, then finds it has an appetite for more. Quickly it begins to devour the extremities and work its way from my flesh to my heart and ultimately my soul. The cold brings pain that is both new and excruciating. A simple tingle gives way to burning that seems so odd in these temperatures, and yet the mind wants to believe the warmth is real. Soon the bones in my hands, arms, feet, and legs throb viciously from the pain as the fluid in my joints seems to simply freeze and refuse to operate. Dread creeps into my mind as I remember how much fatigue I will feel later today from an involuntary response of shivering in order to create even a tiny amount of heat so that I might survive until the heat truck comes by.

Over the thunderous roar of the wind I can hear an almost inaudible purr of a diesel engine propelling the HUMMVEE and its precious commodity of heat to my position. I close my eyes and try to imagine the acrid smell of the vehicle's exhaust stinging my nose in a vain attempt to divert my mind from the cold. I keep feeling something will keep me from going into deep shock when I crawl into the truck for warmth. I try harder now to imagine the warmth of the vehicle's heater and how the heat will wash over my body as it laps at the warmth like a starving dog devouring a dish of freshly ground chuck. It is hard to imagine this could be better than sex, but there is definitely lust in my heart for this sultry, sensuous heat and the pleasure it will bring.

The commander has ordered the truck to rotate to each watch position so that every man can have a mere ten minutes of warmth on his watch tour. Hail, Oh Great Commander! I don't see his face out here for only ten minutes of relief, but I gladly accept the warmth. I am lucky because my position is close to the middle of the rotation, and my relief divides my watch in half making it almost bearable. The poor slobs at the beginning and the end of the rotation get next to no relief at all.

As the truck crawls ever so slowly towards my position, I try to block out the merciless cold with my thoughts. I wonder if this is what death is really like? Darkness so complete it cannot be broken. Cold so deep you feel nothing. To be this empty and lonely in the middle of an army makes me feel like one of the aimless tumbleweeds of the desert southwest, moving without will or destination and serving no real purpose in life.

There are times in my life that I can point to and say were definite turning points. This is one of those times. As I sat on guard duty on the perimeter of my unit's camp in the Saudi Arabian desert, I came to a realization. It was not sudden and there was no flash of light to accompany such a great revelation. This place would always be special to me because here I learned how futile war is for one man. War may serve a purpose for countries and nations, but for the solitary man the only purpose it serves is a lonely death. I don't recall ever hearing a dead man tell how glorious giving his life for his country was, and I know that I never will. For me, the sharing involved with interactions between family and friends is the secret to life. I never want to feel like a tumbleweed blowing in the wind again and hope no person alive has to either.

-Spoon River College, Macomb Campus
Diane M. Taylor, Instructor

I Am More
Victoria Mohatt
(Buffalo, New York)

I was about six or seven years old when I was first asked a question that meant nothing at the time. Now that I understand racism, I understand why it seems to mean everything to everyone. I was asked, "What are you? Black or white?" My mother is black and my father is white, but it had never occurred to me that this situation was different or even unusual, as my neighborhood is racially mixed. I had grown up thinking I was a normal child who wanted nothing more out of life than to be loved, and I was.

I was visiting my grandfather for the summer, far away from my home and the variety of races that I was accustomed to. My grandfather's hometown is a small, underpopulated one, out in the country. Where I lived was just the opposite—a city full of people of different cultures. I had a lot to learn.

There I was at a swimming pool in a town with no cultural diversity. Everyone at the pool was white, including my grandfather. After seeing a little girl with my mother, who is black, and my father, who is white, a little girl became confused when she heard me call them "Mommy and Daddy." Even though I have light skin like my father, I have always been the spitting image of my mother.

The little girl took the chance to ask me about "what" I was when she saw me sitting alone. When she asked me her question, I sat in amazement. Before I could even answer, she ran away scared when she saw my mother coming.

After I pulled myself together from the shock and confusion of her running away, I was surprised to realize that I didn't know the answer to her question.

21

I was so used to seeing different people in my neighborhood, in my school, and in my own home, I figured that I and my family were normal and never questioned or realized the dramatic differences in my parents. The only thing I knew for sure was that they were Mom and Dad who loved and took care of me.

Neither of my parents had really educated me about my roots. Maybe they thought I was too young and race definitions too complex. I turned to my mother and asked her, "What am I? Black or white?" She replied that I had a choice. At that moment, I wanted to be like everyone else, and, since everyone around me was white, I chose to be white; but I would never forget that I had been given a choice.

Now that I look back, I feel that my mother's answer was the wrong one. I am not one or the other; I am both. I cannot deny one-half of myself or whole generations of family history. People who are a part of me and who made me what I am today cannot be erased by a simple, meaningless word, "black" or "white."

People still ask me what I consider myself to be. Race is such a big issue in America. Everyone, no matter who, has been judged at one time or another in terms of race. It seems that everyday I am judged, but since I grew up going to very diverse schools, I have been somewhat accepted by different races.

If I had gone to a predominantly white or black school and only had the chance to know and be accepted by the majority, everything would be different. In that atmosphere, I would not get the chance to meet people from other cultures, to get to know them, and to give them a chance to get to know and accept me. Since I went to a school that had cultural diversity, I am used to being friends with so many different types of people, learning about them and the way they think.

Having had the chance to get to know all these different cultures, I also know that everyone is judgmental, no matter what race. This makes me expect that everyone is going to judge me and want to categorize me, just as that little girl did at that pool twelve years ago.

I refuse to be categorized. I know two different cultures. I feel I have more inside me, because I am both black and white. All my life I have seen how these two different cultures act and how they are treated. I also feel that I am more. I am not saying that I am above anybody, but I am not beneath anybody for not being a whole of some race. I am more, because I have more experience of race than most people do, as other people have more experience of things that I have not.

White people will never be able to understand how black people feel. They get upset when blacks complain about racism and stereotyping.

feel. They get upset when blacks complain about racism and stereotyping. But racism and stereotyping are something black people experience everyday. The same goes for black people who stereotype whites, because they don't understand, either. What does either group really know about the other? Neither has experienced growing up and having to live the way the other has. I was able to see how each culture was treated, and I can understand how each side feels. Stereotypes are wrong and show a person's ignorance. No one group can be categorized as doing everything the same, as if all members are identical.

Friends, strangers, and associates will never go through what I have been going through my whole life. White people identify with my white side, and black people identify with my black side. Each excludes a part of me that makes me who I am and makes me different.

Each time people comment on either race, they are putting me down. But since they have to categorize me, they don't feel that they are putting me down; they consider me to be one or the other—black or white. When someone categorizes me and puts down one or the other race that person is disrespecting either my father or my mother.

The fact that everyone wants to categorize me affects me deeply, because for many of us, there is no one term for all the races one might be. Many of us are "mixed" and have different cultures in our family's history. Why should it matter, anyway, or affect who will accept me or not accept me? In the end, I will prove that I am different from those who want to categorize and stereotype me. I am more.

-Buffalo State College
Sharon Gerring, Instructor

II

Writing to Inform or Explain

The writers of the essays in this chapter each focus on a particular subject, exploring it in some detail in order to share their knowledge of the subject with readers who are not as well-informed as the writer. Sometimes the writer's knowledge about the subject grows out of personal experience, sometimes it is based in research, and sometimes it comes from both personal experience and research. Research sources include print materials, such as books and periodicals, as well as electronic sources accessed through the Internet. What all the essays share is an obvious interest—even excitement—about the subject on the part of the writer, along with a clear purpose of explaining the subject to increase the readers' understanding of it.

As with the personal experiences explored in Chapter I, the range of subjects written about in this chapter is broad. The first two essays here both describe how to do something. In "With My Foot?," Joe Richter explains the basics of playing footbag (or hackey sack), an emerging sport in which players catch and balance a leather bag on the ends of their toes; he both defines the game and details the process for executing one of its basic moves. Next, Richard Black explores the finer points of hitchhiking, offering specific advice for would-be "thumbers" ("Thumbnail Guide to Hitchin' a Ride"). Focusing on a more serious topic, Kenneth Coffman in "The Word Written in Blood" compares and contrasts two revolutions—the American Revolution of the 1700s and the Iranian Revolution of earlier in this century—in order to define the concept of revolution in a historical context. In "Never Fool with Mother Nature," Erin Dernal writes about three kinds of natural disasters—floods, hurricanes, and tornados—using examples drawn from personal experience as well as the media in order to compare the relative destructive power of each.

Andrew Brown's "What Do You Want To Be When You Grow Up?" was written in response to an assignment that asked students to investigate subjects of genuine practical and personal interest and to write their papers as a "what-I-did-and-what-I-found-out" narrative report; Brown, who chose to investigate disk-jockeying as a possible career, composed his essay as an irreverent personal report that is nonetheless cleverly informative. Also writing in a personal style, Jamie Clark explains and defines what kidney disease is, how it is treated, and the toll is takes on patients. In her more traditionally structured research paper "For Want of a Potato," Susan Litzinger explores the causes and effects of the Great Irish Famine of 1845 to 1851, when a potato blight led to starvation at home and the first great wave of Irish immigration to the United States.

The two final papers in this chapter are also based on research. In "The End of Innocence," Kim Smith relies on a number of local sources to trace the rise and decline of railway travel through her small Tennessee town, exploring an interrelated sequence of causes and effects. And Wanda Husted uses a variety of sources—including a number from the World Wide Web— to explore causes in "Why Aren't There More Female Computer Scientists?"

Representing an interesting variety of voices and research and writing strategies, these examples suggest the many possibilities for essays whose primary purpose is to inform or explain.

With My Foot?

Joe Richter
(Dallas, Texas)

Have you ever wondered what it might be like to be able to catch and balance a ball on the tip of your toe? Many footbag (or hackey sack) players would be able to sympathize with you if you have. Hackey sack is a physically demanding sport, which requires intense mental concentration as well. The game can be played alone or with a group of people. The only objective of the game in its purest form is to juggle the footbag (a leather ball that is slightly larger than a golf ball) using only the feet. Many people are involved in the sport, almost daily practicing complicated tricks such as the Pendulum, the Butterfly, the Paradox Mirage, and the Clipper Kick. The art of catching and balancing the sack on your toe is known as a Toe Stall and is really a lot easier than it sounds.

Just as in any sport, using the proper equipment is important in hackey sack. Beginners would do well to start with a quality footbag. The original footbags consisted of two leather panels (both shaped like the numeral eight) sewn together and stuffed with small plastic beads. Modern footbags consist of up to ninety-two panels made of ultra-suede (a durable, soft, leather-like material), sewn together and filled with anything from sand to small polyurethane beads. Players have found that using footbags with a large number of panels results in more consistent reaction to kicks (since the bag will more uniformly deform when struck with the shoe). For the beginner, however, a footbag with sixteen to thirty-two panels will be adequate. Footwear varies wildly for hackey sackers, from thongs to deck shoes and hiking boots. But for most people the ordinary tennis shoe is used. Being so common, they are perfect for the beginner.

Since the main goal of hackey sack is to continually kick the footbag, balance and body control must be mastered if you wish to play the sport. Just the act of kicking the footbag requires that one foot be raised off the ground. The foot which remains on the ground (the plant foot) must support the weight of the body, while body position and the arms provide balance. Anyone who begins to play hackey sack seriously will find that a program of running, cycling, or weight training to increase the strength of the leg muscles is necessary in order to improve. But physical training is not the only requirement for playing hackey sack. Intense concentration is also necessary simply because the basic premise of the sport is not normal. The human body is built to allow for the legs and the feet to support our upright position, while the hands and the arms can be used for other tasks. In hackey sack, the legs and feet perform both operations, so in order to play you must be thinking about what your next kick will be and how you will maintain balance as you execute the kick.

Here I'll describe a toe stall on the right foot, the most basic move. (Most of us are right-handed, and I've found that most people are also right-footed!) Starting with your feet spaced about shoulder width apart, simply toss your footbag up to about shoulder height and slightly in front of your body. As the footbag reaches its apex, raise your right leg and bring your right knee up in a line with the path of the footbag. When the footbag begins to descend, start to lower your right leg, accelerating the speed you lower your leg as the footbag gets closer to your foot. As the footbag descends, it should pass just beyond your knee (that is, over your foot). At this point, your main goal is to attempt to make the speed of the descent of your foot as close as possible to the speed at which the footbag is falling in order to provide the bag a soft landing on the top of your foot.

Maintaining body control and concentration in the final moments before the footbag lands on your foot is very important. You must keep your balance; then just as the sack is about to make contact with your foot, lower your entire body by bending the knee of your plant foot (this is sometimes referred to as a 'hop'). This final adjustment should make the downward motion of your foot almost equal to the rate at which the footbag is falling and allow for a soft landing. As the footbag touches your foot, raise your toes to form a cradle and catch the sack on the top of your foot. After the footbag has landed on your foot, simply stop the downward motion of your leg and foot. Now that you have successfully caught the footbag in a toe stall, you can hold it on your foot for as long as you can maintain your balance and concentration.

Hackey sack is a thoroughly enjoyable sport that teaches superb body control, coordination, and concentration. The tricks that can be performed by experts are incredible to watch (and seemingly impossible). The materials that are required to start playing the sport are minimal so that anyone who wants to can take part. Since the activity is so different from what most people are accustomed to, you will need a lot of practice if you want to become proficient. But a beautiful, sunny afternoon in the park practicing new tricks with your footbag is one of the most pleasant outings that you can undertake.

-Collin County Community College
Sherill Cobb, Instructor

Thumbnail Guide to Hitchin' a Ride
Richard Black
(Cobden, Illinois)

You used to see them on nearly every entrance ramp, on interstates all over the country—their back-packs, duffel bags, old ladies, and dogs strewn around them like so much flotsam—thumb out or holding a sign: dressed in their blue jeans, tie-dyed T-shirts, and sandals and sporting psy-key-delic granny glasses; hair tied up in a ponytail or hanging free down their back, hitchhikers looking for that rainbow's end with the pot of gold. The late-sixties, early-seventies answer to hobos and rail riders, they were the footloose equivalent of gypsy nomads, wandering the highways of America; hitchin' a ride, going somewhere, sometimes anywhere.

For three years and some untold thousands of miles, I was a member of that nomadic group, always heading down the highway, always going over the next hill. From New York to California, Washington to Florida, and most of what lies in between, I wandered the highways, seeing America from the side of the road from the passenger window of rolling vehicles. Hitchin' a ride.

There is an art to flagging down the odd automobile, tractor-trailer rig, "Flat-bed Ford," or transmogrified rendition of any of the above. This is why a lot of those long-haired thumbers I described earlier sometime spent days lolling about the greasy sides of on-ramps—and a helluva lot less time moving down the highway—while I and Tom Robbins' Sissy Hankshaw were busy breaking cross-country travel records. It is actually possible to make it from New York to California by thumb faster than the average person can make it driving. It's all in how you waggle that digit, friends, and all in how you present yourself while doing it.

One of the most important things to remember when hitch-hiking is to appear relaxed. Someone who looks tense does not instill receptiveness on the part of your average driver. I can't tell you how many times I've caught rides with people who just got finished not giving some poor slob a ride, only to find out that they failed to do so because they thought the other person seemed a little too high strung. So, take it easy.

My favorite stance was always one of near sloughing, arm dangling almost limply at my side, thumb casually thrown out over an open hand, eyes front, with a noncommital look on my face. It is amazing how many people, of varying backgrounds and origins, will stop to give you a lift when they think you're not really in any hurry to get somewhere.

Now, Sissy Hankshaw had an advantage that your average hitchhiker couldn't compete with, in addition to the fact that she was an attractive member of the female gender. As Tom Robbins so eloquently puts in his book, *Even Cowgirls Get the Blues*, "It is a thumb. The thumb. The thumbs, both of them. It is her thumbs that we remember, it is her thumbs that have set her apart." They were, in a word, huge. Overripe tomatoes of thumbs, that could catch a motorist's eye from a quarter mile or more away. Unable to compete with her anatomy, we are forced to use other, more inventive measures to solicit the ride we seek.

The open hand catches the eye, but does more than that. In ways that only psychologists can adequately explain, it also reassures. Much like the salute, the hitchhiker with the hand held out, fingers slightly turned up, almost supplicating, will be recognized and returned the favor. The relaxed stance also serves to put drivers at ease, giving you the appearance of someone who is unthreatening, harmless.

The biggest mistake, by far, that your average hitchhiker makes though, is traveling with everything he or she owns. It's not just the quality of your appearance that gets you those rides; it is also the quantity. Here's another reason why those long-haired friends of mine spent so much time sitting on the grass instead of rolling down the highway. The more "stuff" you have with you on the road, the fewer vehicles *can* carry you, let alone will.

Most of my early career hitchin' rides—that is my teen years, when it was my need to hitch across state to see various girls and the like—I traveled extremely light, usually with just the clothes on my back. It made for some interesting weekends, to say the least, but it served me well.

Later, when I knew I was going to be, in effect, living off the road, I carried a back-pack, in which I carried a couple pair of jeans, some cutoffs, assorted socks, toiletries, and a couple of paperbacks. For a time, I also carried a journal with my poems in it. Tied to the bottom of the pack was my sleeping bag. That was it. That was all I needed.

Of course, I no longer feel the urge to wander down the highways via the opposing digit of my right hand. For one thing, it's too damn dangerous out there. But, mostly, I just don't have the stamina for it anymore. The years have softened me, and—I'm not embarrassed to admit it—I rather like getting where I'm going in my own car, at my own pace. I still like to feel the road flowing underneath me, I just prefer to see it passing away from the security of my own rearview mirror.

Some years back I happened upon a book by Douglas Adams, The *Hitchhiker's Guide to The Universe*. It intrigued me to think that one day it might be possible to wander the Universe with the same freedom that I once wandered the great American road system. However, for the time being anyway, it appears that it won't be an easy task to undertake. Take, for instance, the following excerpt:

> *People often ask me how they can leave the planet, so I have prepared some brief notes.*

How to Leave the Planet

> *1.   Phone NASA. Explain that it's very important that you get away as soon as possible.*
>
> *2.   If they do not cooperate, phone any friend that you may have in the White House...to have a word on your behalf with the guys at NASA.*
>
> *3.   If you don't have any friends in the White House, phone the Kremlin. They don't have any friends there either (at least, none to speak of), but they do seem to have a little influence, so you may as well try.*
>
> *4.   If that also fails, phone the Pope for guidance.. I gather his switchboard is infallible.*
>
> *5.   If all these attempts fail, flag down a passing flying saucer and explain that it's vitally important that you get away before your phone bill arrives.*

It would be a good idea to try and brush up on your hitchhiking abilities as well because soliciting one of those rides is something you can do only about once a millennia or so.

-Southeast Missouri State University
Mike Hogan, Instructor

The Word Written in Blood

Kenneth R. Coffman

The French philosopher Simon Weil, once wrote, "The word 'revolution' is a word for which you kill, for which you die, for which you send the laboring masses to their death, but which does not possess any content." Indeed, many people deem the word *revolution* to mean different things. Compton's Reference Collection states that a revolution is to "overthrow a government, form of government, or social system by those governed and usually by forceful means, with another government or system taking its place." My history professor has stated that "a revolution is a radical movement, the purpose of which is to bring about fundamental changes in economic, social, and political systems." I believe them all, but I also believe that revolutions do not always abide by these definitions. The American and Iranian revolutions serve as two good examples.

The American Revolution began on April 19, 1775, when British regulars fired on the Minutemen of Lexington, Massachusetts. This shot was heard around the world. On October 19, 1781, the revolution ended with the surrender of the British at Yorktown. The Iranian Revolution started in 1951, when the Majlis tried to force the Shah of Iran into a position of a constitutional monarch. On January 16, 1979, the revolution finally ended when the Shah left the country. Did these revolutions cause any of the fundamental changes referred to in the previous definitions? I think they did in the Iranian Revolution and did not in the American Revolution.

During the American Revolution, the colonists' economic beliefs and systems changed little. The colonists always believed in the systems of free trade and mercantilism, and kept these systems alive long after the revolutionary period. They did not believe in direct taxation, and they maintained this position for years to come. On the other hand, the Iranian Revolution brought about colossal economic changes. During the revolutionary period in the 1950s, the prime minister of Iran's government nationalized Iran's oil and forced the withdrawal of the British Oil Company. Unemployment went unchecked and ran rampant throughout the country. Revolutionaries destroyed cities along with homes and businesses alike, further deepening the gashes of revolution. In 1963 the Shah declared the White Revolution. This subrevolution broke the powers of the large landowners, an action which led to the distribution of land to the people who had never before owned any. This subrevolution also called for the nationalization of forests, public sale of state-owned industries, and several other concessions in an attempt to pacify the revolutionaries. These changes drastically affected the economic outlook

31

for Iran, and foreigners were no longer interested in investing in Iran. The wealthy people of Iran, who had their land stolen from them, would now be equally resistant to the reigning government.

Socially, few changes occurred during the American Revolutionary period. The colonists took steps toward the separation of church and state, the granting of greater religious freedoms, and women gaining more respect within the community; they now denounced the granting of titles of nobility and privileges based on birth. Overall, few ordinary people wanted radical changes, and thus, little social upheaval was evident. Unlike the colonists, the Iranians had tremendous social turmoil. The government's failure to guarantee civil and political rights led to widespread demonstrations, the death of many people, and the imposition of martial law. The government executed hundreds of Iranians for political and/or religious reasons, and imprisoned or forced thousands more into exile merely for speaking their beliefs. The militants did not confine the fighting to the battlefields; it took place in the cities and towns, on playgrounds and streets. The people were not immune from the effects of this revolution.

Perhaps the greatest change of a revolution is the radical change in political systems. During the colonization of America, the settlers had become accustomed to taking a share in the government. Every colony elected an assembly much like England's Parliament. The Virginians set up their House of Burgesses only twelve years after they settled Jamestown. The Pilgrims drew up the Mayflower Compact before building their first log cabin. The colonists had these sets of rule for governing their colonies, and they based them upon their original charters from King George III. During the revolution, the colonists were framing state constitutions even before they signed the Declaration of Independence, and they also based these constitutions upon their colonial charters. The colonists did not seek any fundamental changes in the political system of America during the revolution. In fact, Connecticut and Rhode Island continued to operate under their English charters well into the nineteenth century. They never toppled the political system of England, nor did they try.

Unlike the American Revolution, the Iranian Revolution produced tremendous political changes. A council led by a longtime opponent to the Shah of Iran took control of the government. The Shah escaped from his country with his life, and the Ayatollah came back out of exile to declare Iran an Islamic Republic. The people of Iran looked to the Ayatollah for greater freedom, fairer distribution of wealth, and a government that followed the teachings of Islam. They received none. The coalition of forces that helped overthrow the Shah collapsed. Militant Islamic revolutionaries took over the country, these militants overthrew the nationalists and their leaders including the elected president. While the Ayatollah still had considerable power as their spiritual leader, they were in fact a country without a government. With some haphazard attempts of coordination from the Ayatollah, the military factions controlled the destiny of Iran.

The American Revolution was hardly a classical example of a revolution as defined earlier. The colonists who fought the American Revolution sought to preserve their economic, social, and political ways, not to change them. The Iranians on the other hand, fought for a different way of government and life altogether, a true revolution as generally defined.

-*Central Texas College*
Donny Yeilding, Instructor

Never Fool With Mother Nature

Erin Demel
(Allen, Texas)

I was only eleven at the time, but I remember it so vividly. The winds started howling. The rain, combined with small pieces of hail, came down in sheets. The sky was pitch black, almost the color of tar. On the horizon, clear sky could be seen, but it seemed to be millions of miles away. My nostrils filled with the smell of dirt and rain-soaked roads. My hair matted to my face, and my clothes stuck to my body from the rain. My shoes were even full of water. Worst of all, ants and spiders crawled up and down my legs as I forced myself even further into the culvert to escape the inevitable storm. Over the bodies of my two closest friends and their mother, I could see the rain as it poured down. Then, like a blessing from God, it stopped. My heart ceased its fast-paced rhythm and my muscles relaxed. I heard myself ask, "Can we go now?" To my dismay the reply from my friend was drowned out by the sound of a freight train. As my tears combined with the rain on my face, I heard the tornado roar over the road I was under and destroy every tree in its path. Then, we heard nothing but silence. It was the most beautiful sound in the world. On the short drive home, I wondered if my beloved dogs would still be alive and if my belongings, especially my house, were still intact. To my relief, this incredible storm jumped over my house as if the tornado were a rabbit. Not even a blade of grass was out of place! Unfortunately, my neighbor's roof was damaged, and his beloved cat was missing. It was at this time that I first contemplated the cruelty of nature. Every natural disaster known to man is just that: a disaster. Many people lose their belongings, their homes, their pets, and even their lives to these bizarre acts of nature. Three natural disasters that are particularly devastating are floods, hurricanes, and tornados.

Most people don't view a little rain as a natural disaster. Normally, it is not. Consider what would happen if an area received many relentless days of rain and snow. After a while, the ground becomes so saturated that the rain that is falling has nowhere to go. Therefore, it collects and builds until it begins to flood the area. The Midwest recently battled this natural disaster. Many people decided to brave out this period of torrential rainfall but were forced to leave once the water became too high. For example one gentleman and his family decided to stay in the home that had been in his family for fifty years. When the water got too high, he moved his family to the second floor of his home. When the water began to seep through the floor of his second story, he moved his family to the roof. At that time, the National Guard rescued him and his family and took them to shelter. Last week, he returned to his home alone. He wanted to assess the damage before he brought his family to see it. At first, he was stunned by what he saw: damaged furniture, missing walls, and even a duck in his kitchen sink. Then he became angry. With tears rolling down his face, he shook his fist at the heavens and screamed, "Why did you do this to me?" These floods have not only destroyed his home, they have destroyed his life. Floods are so devastating because they destroy homes and leave people stranded. Floods also destroy power lines and telephone lines, thereby obliterating all lines of communication. Fortunately, this natural disaster does have a nemesis, unlike most other forms of natural disaster. Dams and dikes can be built to protect low-lying areas and the people who live there. Unfortunately for the people in the Midwest, nothing was done to protect them and their treasured possessions.

Another form of natural disaster is the hurricane. A hurricane builds in the ocean and gains speed and intensity as it approaches land. This is fortunate for the people in its path because meteorologists can usually predict when and where the hurricane will hit. In order to remember these natural disasters, they are given human names such as Andrew, Frank, and even Erin. When a hurricane hits land, it brings winds in excess of a hundred miles per hour, incredible rainfall, and deadly lightening. It can also cause power outages, flooding, and even tornados. When Hurricane Andrew hit Florida several years ago, my uncle was there visiting some friends., Unfortunately, he was unable to retreat to a safe location, so he was stranded in their beach-front home in the middle of this storm. As he took shelter in a closet, he could hear the wind ripping apart the roof and their belongings being thrown throughout their house. Unlike a tornado, this storm lasted for almost an hour. When he was finally able to come out, he was shocked at the amount of damage that high winds and rain could cause to a house. Several thousand dollars were spent on the repairs to that house only to be hit by another hurricane a year later. Like floods, hurricanes also destroy homes and people's lives. They also obliterate any form of communication with those not affected by the hurricane. In addition, they tend to hit one area over and over again. Fortunately, a hurricane also has a nemesis. Since hurricanes are easily tracked, people can prepare their houses for the attack of this storm and then retreat to a safe place. Human lives lost in a hurricanes are less than those lost in tornados, but the damage is still great. After all, you can protect your home from the winds and the rain, but you cannot move it out of its path.

The scariest natural disaster is the tornado. Tornados usually hit with little or no warning. Also, a tornado's path is always random. It may destroy one house, but never even touch the one next to it. A tornado usually brings heavy rains and hail, but it always brings extremely high winds that move in a circular motion. It also destroys everything in its path. I have even heard of a tornado forcing a piece of straw through a tree stump! In the movie *Twister*, the main characters have just survived an F-5 tornado, or the worst tornado known to man. As they look across the horizon, they notice every barn and house that has been destroyed except for one lonely house in the distance that has not even been scratched. This is very typical of a tornado. For example, my friend owns a house in Wylie, Texas. On Mother's Day in 1993, a tornado ripped through that town, devastating everything in its path. My friend's house lost a few shingles from its roof, but was otherwise unscathed. Her neighbor's house was leveled to the foundation. The people of Wylie also had little warning that a tornado was even on its way. Fortunately, few lives were lost, but the property damage was extreme. Currently, no nemesis exists for a tornado. In fact, because of its random nature and the fact that it gives little warning, people faced with a tornado can only protect themselves and are forced to let their belongings, homes, and even their pets bear the brunt of this storm. This makes a tornado the most frightening natural disaster known to man.

When I emerged from the culvert that rainy, spring day, the first thing I noticed was the beautiful rainbow in the sky. My first thought was how beautiful nature is and how lucky I am to be able to enjoy it. Then I began to look at my neighborhood and the devastation that a simple act of nature caused. For the most part, Mother Nature treats us very well by giving us beautiful trees, fields covered in blue bonnets, and gorgeous waterfalls. Every once in a while, Mother Nature becomes "angry" and unleashes her wrath. Unfortunately, we are forced to pick up the pieces and begin again after Mother Nature has finished her business. Until we can find a way to control this savage beast side of Mother Nature, we will be forced to recover and move on. Luckily for us, Mother Nature can destroy our physical items, but she cannot take away our spirit.

-Colin County Community College
Sherill Cobb, Instructor

What Do You Want to be When You Grow Up?

Andrew Brown
(Cookeville, Tennessee)

Some people know what they want to do with their lives. They seem to have known since they popped from the womb. My mom, for example, always wanted to be a nurse. She never even thought about a different career. On the other hand, my dad still hasn't found something that makes him happy, or rich, unfortunately. I'm nineteen, with no idea what to do with my life, but with the conviction that I don't want to turn out like him, aimless and disgruntled at fifty.

I am, at best, a slacker. At worst, I'm lazy. If I owned a TV, I'd never leave my apartment. I am Generation X incarnate. I listen to music twenty-four hours a day, including while I'm sleeping, interrupted only by the occasional class that I wake up for. I fiddle around with my computer, basically blasting aliens on video games. I have heard that there are other things you can do with a computer, but I haven't found anything that counts as a skill, unless you regard finding porn in the internet as career-making expertise. That might count if I'm elected to Congress, but otherwise I'm on my own.

I've spent two years at a job I barely like. I only still work there because I do not really do anything and I do not have to be nice to people. I work at a movie theater, starting the shows. It takes real skill to press the start button, wait two hours, and then press it again. But I don't take any lip from the customers, and my boss even thinks it's funny when I am rude. I have been fired from jobs for less than I do on a daily basis at the theater. There was the time I laughed at one boss when he announced with sincerity that the customer was always right, and then announced that I was no longer needed. Of course, if you wanted to see ornery, you should have seen me at Papa John's. No wonder I never received any tips.

What can a person like me do for a living? I have no job skills, people skills, encouragable skills, or luck. I am mean, or at least unsociable, shiftless, and uncharismatic, not to mention my physical shortcomings. I do have a quick wit, however sarcastic it might be, and I can make anybody laugh if I try. Hasn't stopped me from getting beat up a lot, but it is all I have to work with on short notice.

College has not been much help. My advisor keeps telling me to take stupid general classes on subjects I hate, so "when (I) do pick my major, (I) will have these classes out of the way." My question is, how can I decide on a major if I only take classes that don't interest me? Isn't the whole idea behind school finding something I like doing? How can I do that when I'm taking crap? If I hated math throughout grade school, what is supposed to change my mind now? Of course, my advisor and I do not see eye to eye, so I am forced to visit her office every other day. I have been there six times at last count, and I overheard her mumble "Oh no, it's him again," last time I went to see her. But I'm wearing her down and getting things my way. So I'll probably be here seven years, so what. I didn't have anything better to do.

This semester, I did find something that interests me. In between the pencil-pushing bureaucrats in the advisement department and the endless hours of boredom in worthless classes, I found WTTU. For those of you that don't know—and that's about three-fourths of the people in the class—WTTU is the college radio station here at Tech. Basically, you put your name on the X and agree not to curse too much and, bam, you're a DJ. It is fun. I play the music that I like. Program Manager be damned, and I get to be mean to people on the air. What more could I ask for? But how could I make a career out of it, and would I want to?

⁖

I figured that the easiest place to find out how to become a DJ was to go straight to the source and ask some DJ's. They should know, since they are on the air. And I wanted to know how they broke into the industry, whether it was worth it, what it paid, and the most important question, were there DJ groupies for the taking?

The first place I called was Kicks 106.9. I was unimpressed. The moron robot secretary I talked to, whose name was not worth remembering, told me they did not "endorse interviews" (her words, not mine). If I could get a hold of a DJ on my own, that was fine, but it was not her job to set up an appointment. I have since erased 106.9 off my radio's pre-selected channels. I have a friend named Ray who works at Kicks, but the only time I remembered to ask him I got some unintelligible sentence about computers and Toto. I've heard Ray on those rare Sunday mornings that I'm up before noon, and I can see why he is only on Sunday mornings. Door One closed.

Then I ran into Deena, the program director at WTTU, who herself once worked at Kicks, but felt it was too fake. For every question I threw her way, I got an answer that suggested her loathing of commercial radio. "I love our DJs because they make mess-ups. I remember...I wish they would just mess up once...you know those commercial DJs...I mean it's just so perfect all the time. Since I started working on college radio, I've yet to listen to any of that (commercial radio) because it's just too fake."

You would think a question like "what is the major difference between college DJs and commercial DJs" would be harmless right? Wrong.

"Our DJs are here because they really like the music, not because

37

they're getting paid. I mean if you work at a commercial radio station, you have absolutely no choice at all. The music director lays it all out. Those DJs don't get a choice of what they play at all. They might like it. The fake laughs, though, I can't stand the fake laughs."

I am so glad I taped her responses. I only wish I hadn't recorded over her a week later in Nashville. The tape would have provided blackmail if she ever becomes famous. She did give me my first real doubts about a career in the music industry, regardless. If she felt that strongly about it, maybe there was something against commercial radio.

I did receive some useful information. She made a reference to Chad, who now works at Sunny 95 point something or other, but used to work at WTTU. I called that station, and they were happy to give me his shift times. I told them what time to expect me and I was all set for Saturday night.

I did what I never thought I'd do: set foot in a country music station. If I have it my way, I'll never set foot in one again. It was not a hideous as I thought, but it was bad enough. A full color poster of Garth Brooks adorned the front lobby, and signed pictures of famous country starts lined the hall. At least, I guess they were famous; I wouldn't know. Added to the decorum was the faint whispers of country being piped from the studio. It was just like I picture hell to be.

Chad seemed nice enough, even though I didn't really get any good information from him. He was around twenty-two or three, with butched hair and glasses—not what I expected for country music, but just right for the alternative played at WTTU. He gave me a basic textbook answer to how to break into the business, mentioning WTTU was a good place to start and all I had to do was send out a lot of resumes and demo tapes and hope I get lucky. Thank you for the vote of confidence, Chad. There was just one question I really had to ask. Why go from alternative music to country? "I get paid."

How much he wouldn't tell me. Things were not looking up for a merry DJ career.

&

I was out of options. I had gone through WTTU and the better part of Cookeville without learning anything. I used the school computers to "surf the net," hoping for some tidbits of information that would help me along my path. Do you know what you get if you look up DJ in the Netscape Navigator? Ninety-seven entries selling private DJs for parties, weddings, and the like, and the Paul Harvey Home Page, which other than answering my question "Just how old is that guy?" did not help me out.

On a whim I called WKDF, a Nashville station that I always listen to. While little radio stations treated me like dirt, the secretary of this major station—one of the most listened-to in Nashville I might add—was helpful and kind. Without any trouble I was able to score an interview with the morning people, Big Dave and the Dook, after their shift.

Going to Nashville was no problem. It was spring break, and since my friends backed out of the Florida trip, I was free for the week, much to my disgust. I left early Wednesday morning, hoping to catch the end of the show. Unfortunately, me being as bad with directions as I am and Nashville traffic being as bad as it is, I was about five minutes late. I hurtled up the stairs three at a time, on my way asking directions from every person with a mop. But I reached them before they left.

They were very bizarre, to say the least. Big Dave—Dave to his friends since that's his name—was tall and lanky, with glasses and a quick wit. The Dook—which is pronounced—Duke—was shorter and little huskier, with glasses and a deep laugh. They reminded me of Johnny Carson and Ed McMahon. I asked if it was OK to use my tape recorder and Dook, whose real name is Doug, gave a comment that really summed up a good DJ's personality:

"I get nervous around microphones."

After that joke had sunk in, I had a very witty conversation with two very amusing men.

They answered my questions, more or less. If I want to find work, I'm going to have to send out demo tapes and resumes. I had hear that before, but when colorful commentary about a hick Alabama station was added by Dave, the information seemed clearer. "I took this God-awful job in Alabama. They said it was rock and pop. Turned out to be Skynyrd and Steve Miller. Of course, for rural Alabama, that was pop. Listen to the station you're going to work for before taking a job." I also learned never to take the first job offer I received, but not to reject it either. "I finally felt the urge to go postal after about three months. I dropped the job when my sanity couldn't stand it. Of course, since I had turned down my other offers, I was living on Roman noodles for a few weeks."

Groupies? "Oh yeah, they're all over the place. We have to beat them off with a stick."

"Break out the cattle prods," Dook/Doug remarked,

"We have to fight them off every morning to get into the station," smirked Dave.

OK. No DJ groupies. I expected that, but in the bottom of my heart and head, I prayed differently. I could live with that, now show me the money.

"Money? We're supposed to be getting paid?" Dave chimed in with more of his clever repartee. "We get almost enough to afford a cardboard box on Fourth Avenue. As long as we don't make any phone calls, eat anything extravagant, or anything like that."

I had a good time. I also learned that if I was serious, a really good place to go was MTSU. It has an excellent communications program and intern program. I also need to find a station that plays music I like, because I'll have to play it. I'll also have to pretend that I like it, even though I think it's garbage. Right now, if I don't like a song, I'll say it, make fun of it while it's playing, or if it's really hideous, cut it off. That's half the fun of being a DJ.

ɞ

I still did not have enough information. I had talked to enough people, and I was getting sick of it. It was time to break down and read something. But where to find a book on Disc Jockeying. The library was no help. After an hour of looking for books that did not help, I felt like piling the books in a stack and starting a 1984-style bonfire. Luckily, after explaining my dilemma to my friend Michael, he told me he had just the thing. He was right. The King of all Radio. Howard Stern, had a book that, after sifting through the offensive nonsense, had many useful tidbits.

One thing I noticed about being a DJ is that it involves moving a lot. Dave went from Alabama to Mississippi to Kentucky and now he's here in Nashville for who knows how long. Stern went from Boston to Detroit to Washington D.C. to New York and finally to Los Angeles. Do I want to do all that moving around? I want to get out of Cookeville, but not travel the countryside. When I find someplace I like to be, I stay there.

The big question for me is, do I want to be a DJ? If so, I believe I know how, but only I can answer the question of whether or not I should make a career out of it. Could I spend my life listening to music? I do now, but I'm still maturing. At least I hope I'm still maturing. I learned a lot by writing this paper, but at the same time I've learned nothing.

-Tennessee Technical University
Michael O'Rourke, Instructor

As Time Ticks By

Jamie Clark
(Nashville, Tennessee)

Kidney is either of a pair of glandular organs in vertebrates, which separate waste products from the blood and excrete them as urine (New World Dictionary 412).

Sandy climbed into the back seat of a yellow cab in downtown New York, and directed the cab driver to the airport. He was a dark, hairy man named Jock. There has to be a reason why a guy named Jock is a cab driver, she thought, but that was too personal. He started to tell of the time he had to go to the airport to drop off his wife Ellen. She flew out to California to care for her sickly mother, Kathleen. She had been diabetic ever since he and Ellen were married. This disease strained her kidneys. It was amazing how Jock could do so many things at one time: drive, smoke, wave gestures to fellow cabbies, swerve in and out of lanes, and tell an impressive story.

Dialysis is the separation of crystalloids from colloids in solution by the greater diffusability of the smaller molecules through a semipermeable membrane. Dialyze is to undergo dialysis (New World Dictionary 208).

Kathleen lived with her husband of fifty years, and could barely make it around their two-story cape cod before being hospitalized for renal failure. When Ellen arrived at the hospital, Kathleen was drained of her spirits, her blood, and her willpower. She had been on dialysis for most of the day. This procedure took place every other day or so. She was hooked up to a dialysis machine through a catheter in her arm. The blood, after having been "cleaned," was returned to the body. This cycle is repeated until all of the blood is "clean," and back in the body.

"Nephro" is a combining form meaning Kidney. "Ology" means the study of. Nephrology means the study of kidney(s) (New World Dictionary 502).

The National Kidney Foundation meeting that kidney specialist Dr. Sandy Hedgepath was almost certainly going to be late to, because of New York traffic, was to be held in Houston, Texas. Nephrologists would talk about new surgical techniques, donor recipient lists, patients, and time. *Time*. Will some of these patients die before the spotlight is on them? Before they find a match? Before they receive their kidney? These are questions that run through Sandy's mind everyday.

"Okawhena" means kidney in Indian.

Camp Okawhena, or "kidney camp," is a place were people ages 5-18 with kidney problems can go for seven out of 365 days to do things that normally they would not or could not do. They meet new friends in better or worse condition than themselves and share experiences. This week helps them appreciate their life and the lives of others.

Antigen is a substance to which the body reacts by producing antibodies (New World Dictionary 25). They appear on the cell surface.

Kathleen had been on the transplant recipient list for only a few days. A match was found in her immediate family. In this case, it was not a long drawn-out process. Sometimes a patient will die while waiting for a match. Kathleen was lucky.

Prednazone and Dialanton are two types of antirejection medications that have abnormal effects on the patient. Prednazone often causes an excess amount of hair on the face and arms. A combination of several antirejection medications can result in stunted growth, and perhaps, tumors.

The activities planned for the children at camp are crafts, dances, a trip to Opryland, a talent show, kickball, volleyball, swimming Olympics, and various other sports and games. These activities give them the time to show themselves how talented they are. They do not feel "less important" because they cannot run, jump or swim faster than the other children. They all have more or less the same disabilities that everyone else has.

Hydrocephalic means a person has water surrounding the brain.

I believe that most treatment for illness comes from the mind. It is not the medication that makes a patient better (in some cases), it is what the mind thinks the medication is doing. I also know that these children have renal malfunctions and *must* take their medication or else worse things might happen, such as rejection, or death. But, on the bright side, Camp Okawhena is a place where these children can become mentally stable. Being around other people their own age, having fun, and not worrying has a lot to do with their health, even if it is just one week out of the year.

At camp I am "in charge" of Chris Mincey. He is an eighteen-year-old, mildly retarded, hydrocephalic kidney-transplant patient. I give him his daily doses of medicine and watch over him during the day. He needs help swimming and walking long distances. My days are usually spent with him and other younger children that constantly stay by my side. I don't mind. I do not mind at all.

Most transplant clinics require a two-out-of-six antigen match. The 2a, 2b, 2dr locus of antigens are found on the sixth chromosomes.

I have been a counselor at kidney camp for three years, and a camper for over ten. I have no kidney problems but want to help those kids that do. A big part of my life is being involved with the National Kidney Foundation, because I have known so many people with renal problems. My father also worked for a lab that did the bloodwork for matches and has been affiliated with the NKF ever since. I go to most of their meetings over the summers and walk in their parades distributing donor cards to the people along the street. What I hate to see most while doing this is the reaction of people. Some think that signing a donor card is like handing out a death sentence. It is not this way. You have options! But most people do not want to take the time to learn those options.

At the National Kidney Foundation meeting, the new donor lists of hundreds of patients were distributed for each of the doctors' respective cities. Sandy got to the name Jock Allen Paterson. Could this be the same Jock who entertained her through the madness of downtown New York? Who influenced her life for the short distance to the airport? Will she influence his life? Time choked down on their cab ride, so the conversation was brief. Still, the twenty or thirty minutes of listening to problems and relating his life to her seemed more than just a cab ride. She wanted to help him in his situation. Does time show mercy for anything? Life is delicate, and time shows no mercy.

Works Cited

New World Dictionaries. Simon and Schuster.

Student's Handbook including Webster's New World Dictionary, Vol. 2.
The Southwestern Company: Nashville, TN, 1992.

-Tennessee Technical University
Heidemarie Weidner, Instructor

For Want of a Potato

Susan Litzanger
(Altoona, Pennsylvania)

For want of a nail, the shoe was lost.
For want of a shoe, the horse was lost.
For want of a horse, the soldier was lost.
For want of a soldier, the battle was lost.
For want of the battle, the war was lost.

...Traditional Saying

Between 1845 and 1851 an estimated one million Irish citizens starved to death. An equal number fled Ireland, emigrated to America (Kinealy 295, 297). This national disaster in Irish history resulted from neither war nor pestilence. Rather, the seemingly innocuous tuber known today as the "Irish potato" determined this devastating period of Irish economic and sociopolitical life and wrought significant changes in the course of American history as well.

The "Gardener's Chronicle" in 1845 claimed that "4,500,000 persons in Ireland are fed upon Potatoes alone." Potatoes, supplemented by a little milk or butter or, on rare occasions, by a little meat, served as the staff of life for thousands of poverty-stricken peasants in Ireland (Dodge 87, 97). *Solanum tuberosom,* a nearly perfect food, provided plentiful carbohydrates, protein, calcium, niacin, and a considerable amount of Vitamin C. Low in fat and delicious in taste, the potato could be prepared with ease and versatility. It could be stored simply and for long periods of time. No part of the tuber went to waste, not even the water in which it was cooked (Hughes 1,2).

Other advantages made the potato a valuable foodstuff to the Irish peasant. The underground crop more easily escaped the notice of plundering English soldiers and could not be set afire as wheat fields might be. Nor did potatoes need to be taken to a mill to be processed, but could be eaten raw if necessary or simply boiled and eaten (Dodge 86, 87). The potato proved ideal for the long-suffering, poverty-ridden Irish peasants—until "the blight."

In September of 1845 the normally healthy, green leaves of the potato plants all across Ireland began to wilt and turn black. Upon digging the tuber, that part of the plant where excess food is stored, alarmed farmers found black, shriveled, putrid masses. In some cases, plants which aboveground looked green and luxurious yielded similarly rotten and foul-smelling potatoes. Potatoes which had seemed free of defect when dug, decomposed into fetid black masses after storage. Approximately one-half the potato crop of Ireland fell victim to "the blight" (Kinealy 31, 32). A prevailing opinion across the panic-stricken land bemoaned a "curse of God upon Ireland" as the cause of the perishing crops. But the pronouncement of eminent botanists targeted the fungus *Botrytis infestans* as the culprit of the disease, for which there was no known cause or remedy (Dodge 94).

Suddenly, there was nothing to eat in Ireland. Dependent solely on the potato and living in rented cottages on English-owned land, the wretchedly poor Irish peasants possessed few resources to fall back on. Mass starvation resulted over the next five years, as a new fungus each successive year caused widespread potato crop failure throughout Ireland (Miller and Wagner 27). The authors of *Out of Ireland* describe life during "the potato famine":

Thousands of peasants starved to death in their cabins or by the roadsides, their mouths stained green by the grass they had eaten in a vain attempt to stay alive...Still others wandered about, frantically looking for food...

(Miller and Wagner 27, 28)

Fleeing starvation, thousands of Irish citizens emigrated to other countries. Between 1846 and 1851 more than one million Irish crossed the Atlantic under wretched conditions en route to America. Often traveling in steerage, men, women, and children of all ages huddled together without air, without light, wallowing in filth and stench, in what came to be known as "coffin ships." Countless thousands died before reaching America (Miller and Wagner 30, 31).

Although Irish immigrants had been coming to America since colonial times, the influx of such a great number of destitute Irish on American shores made an immediate, and not always positive, impact. Because of the anguish that farming the land had proved in Ireland, most Irish immigrants shunned farming and stayed lumped together in industrial and port cities. Massachusetts, New York, Pennsylvania, and Illinois became the destination for more than half the total Irish population. In cities such as Boston, New York, Philadelphia, and Chicago, the penniless, unskilled refugees took whatever jobs they could find, for any wage (Watts 35, 43). The Irish lived in shacks and faced insults about their "shanty-towns" (Griffin 62, 63). Americans derisively labeled the Irish laborers "paddies," because many of them had been named after St. Patrick. In America the new immigrants encountered derision regarding their dress, their speech, their superstitions, and their religion (McDonnell 54, 55, 58).

Despite its derisive treatment of the Irish immigrants, America needed them. The growing country needed workers. Some historical analysts hold that the American economy of the 1850s would not have survived (let alone expanded) were it not for the plentiful, cheap labor force provided by the Irish immigrants. "Paddies" dug the Erie Canal, built the Brooklyn Bridge, and laid most of the tracks of America's first transcontinental railroad, the Union Pacific. They dug coal in Pennsylvania mines and, along with women and children, went to work in garment factories and as domestic workers (McDonnell 54-60).

In addition to filling America's labor needs, the Irish impacted American life by becoming a leading force for the organization of unions. Often exploited as workers, Irish laborers at first took matters into their own hands, forming secret societies to fight for better working conditions and fair wages. From these beginnings came lawful, organized labor unions, like the Teamsters' Union and the Transport Workers Union, which improved conditions for all workers. (McDonnell 61, 62).

As they became assimilated into American society, Irish Americans involved themselves influentially in the areas of civil service and politics. In police and fire departments they became familiar figures. So many Irish-Americans served as police officers that "paddy wagon" became the term used for the vans that transported prisoners (Greenleaf 61, 62). In the political arena the majority of Irish aligned themselves with the Democratic Party and rose to power in urban areas. Tammany Hall, New York City's "Big Boss" political machinery, became the focal point for Irish domination of America's largest city through the 1860s (McDonnell 65-68).

The potato famine dramatically changed Ireland. Population statistics for 1993 cite Ireland's population as 3.5 million, still well below the pre-famine level ("Ireland"). "For want of a potato," a common and unassuming brown-skinned tuber, the Irish suffered one of the greatest tragedies of their history. Their flight from famine and emigration to America impacted American life and history with a powerful and enduring significance.

Works Cited

Dodge, Bertha S. *Potatoes and People: The Story of a Plant.* Boston: Little Brown, 1970.

Greenleaf, Barbara Kaye. *American Fever: The Story of American Immigration.* New York: Four Winds Press, 1970.

Griffin, William D. *A Portrait of the Irish in America.* New York: Scribner's, 1981.

Hughes, Meredith Sayles, and E. Thomas Hughes. *The Great Potato Book.* New York: Macmillan, 1986.

"Ireland." *1996 Grolier Multimedia*.

Kinealy, Christine. *This Great Calamity: The Irish Famine 1845-52*. Boulder, Colorado: Roberts Rinehart, 1995.

McDonnell, Virginia B. *The Irish Helped Build America*. New York: Julian Messner, 1969.

Miller, Kirby and Paul Wagner. *Out of Ireland: The Story of Irish Emigration to America*. Washington D.C.: Elliot & Clark, 1994.

Watts, J. F. *The Irish Americans*. New York: Chelsea House, 1988.

-Penn State, Altoona Campus
Sandra Petrulionis, Instructor

The End of Innocence
Kim Smith
(Cookeville, Tennessee)

We think of trains as part of the past, and of course they are. They were dirty and a noisy way to travel, but they opened up the world to us. In this essay I will trace the history of trains in the Upper Cumberland area. I will explore the irreversible effect that the "Iron Horse" had on the economic and social growth of the people in this area.

On the fateful day of July 10, 1890, the face of Cookeville and the surrounding area was changed forever. There were over five hundred spectators and a band from Lebanon playing as the first train rolled into Cookeville. The event was called "glorious" by the editor of *The Cookeville Press*, Rutledge Smith, in his July seventeenth issue of the paper (Wallace 4).

That train was met by the old wooden depot that stood for twenty years just slightly east of the brick depot that still stands today. It was built in 1910 by the Tennessee Central Railroad. Laura Copeland, a native of Cookeville, was there to witness the historic event. She boarded the train bound for Cookeville in Carthage where she taught piano lessons. She remembers the train was very crowded with men. She believed them to be from the north because they were ill-mannered and did not get up to offer her a seat (Wallace 3).

What actually brought the railroad to this area were the rich deposits of coal a Pennsylvania businessman, Alexander Crawford, believed were here. He built a railroad from Lebanon to Monterey in order to reach the coal.

It was the ending of innocence and the beginning of progress for the people of the Upper Cumberland (McMillan 2). A writer in the *Smith County Record* wrote in 1885, "Let us begin the new year, set aside resolutions that we will no longer be shut out from the outside world in these mountains, but cry aloud for a railroad" (McMillan 1). These sentiments were echoed by many people of this area.

What it must have been like for the people of Putnam County to sit on the edge of a brand new world! These were extraordinary times for these people! It was scary, exciting, and thrilling for these "mountain people" who had been cut off from much of the world! Many people had never even seen a train before.

Mattie Massa spoke of the first time she ever heard a train. The year was 1898 and she was eight years old. She had just arrived from her farm on Martin's Creek, an eighteen-mile journey that had taken an entire day. She and her brother were visiting her aunt Flora who lived across from the depot. She said, "The train roared, rumbled, shrieked, clanged, and clattered! It ended with an angry hiss! I could not think it was anything except the end of time." She and her brother hid under the bed until the sound had disappeared (McMillan 2).

For the first time in their lives, the people of the Upper Cumberland area were able to reach out and touch faraway places and still have the security of home. Always before they had been confined to the communities they lived in, except for occasional excursions to town or to a relative's house. A twenty-mile trip would take them all day. This is the reason that communities were so much closer in the nineteenth century and the early twentieth century. The social center of most communities was the church. The people had no other social outlet, so church was definitely the place to be. But with the railroads, new avenues were opened. Whoever said "you can't stop progress" was certainly right! Once the railroad came into this area, the future took an inevitable course. For the first time, people could travel to Nashville and still be home in their beds the same night. The same trip a few years before would have taken four or five days one way by horse and buggy!

The people of this area were financially rewarded as well as socially rewarded when the railroad came to town. They sold many different things for profit to the larger cities. Chickens and eggs were very profitable for Putnam County. In fact, Algood became known as "The Chicken Capitol of the World." Farmers also exported tobacco, corn, peas, and farm animals for profit (Delozier 4).

The lives of the farm families changed more drastically than any others. They became more and more dependent on the goods the trains brought in and the money they received for the products they sold. Because of the export of some of their surplus crops, they had more money available to buy "store bought" items that came in on the trains. Some of the store bought items the farmers bought were shoes, piece goods, and men's suits (Delozier 4).

"There was ice cream and freshly baked bread on the noon train to Algood," remembers Mildred Summers (McMillan 1, 2). Apples, oranges, and tangerines always arrived by train during the Christmas season. There was a person on the train called a "butch" who sold gum, fruit, newspapers, and other items. Mrs. Mamie Willis writes, "I can never smell a fresh orange without thinking of trains. Someone was sure to buy an orange…and when the orange was peeled, the sweet, appetizing aroma wafted over the entire length of the car" (Delozier 3).

Hotels and restaurants sprang up to accommodate the passengers of the trains. Cookeville had the Duke House, located directly across from the depot, that served delicious food to travelers and to locals as well. In fact, the Duke House had a doorman who would stand on the front porch of the establishment every evening when the train came in and ring the dinner bell. There is a parking lot where the elegant hotel once stood.

All this new-found abundance was great for towns like Cookeville, but many of the smaller country stores could not complete, and failed. This was sad, of course, for the owners of the stores, but it was also sad for the communities surrounding them. The closing of the stores had an impact economically, but also socially on the communities. The stores were places for neighbors to gather and visit with each other. I see the closing of these country stores as one of the first steps in alienating one neighbor from another in the rural areas.

During this time, Cookeville lost trade to Nashville because of the shopper trains running back and forth. Shopper trains were trains that would pick people up in the rural areas and take them to Nashville, and return them home late the same day. Also, mail order became big and "almost everyone ordered from the Sears and Roebuck 'Wish Book'" according to Aurelia McMurray (Delozier 7).

The social life of the area residents was changed forever. Many people believed it was much improved. No longer was the social life of a person dependent only on the community he or she lived in! People could go to many different places that offered a variety of entertainment. One of the most popular places to go in the summer was Monterey.

Because of its altitude of eighteen hundred feet, Monterey usually had cool summer nights and pleasant days (Delozier 5). It became an elegant resort in the early 1900s. Hensley Williams recalls the "large and tasty" meals served by the luxurious hotels in Monterey. He bought a summer home there and looked forward with "gusto and glee" to the summers! Many people went there to "take the waters," attend concerts, watch ballgames, parades or to attend county fairs among other things (Delozier 10).

Because of the enrichment the railroad brought to their lives, the people in this area loved it. When trains would pass by Algood, the housewives would shake the wash they were hanging out to dry as a friendly greeting. A section of track became known as "Shake Rag" and today is still called "Shag Rag" (McMillan 2).

The depots were like community centers for the townspeople. The old men would quit their whittling and spitting on the sidewalks in order to walk down to the depot so they could see who was coming and going. On Sundays, the town would rush from church to meet the twelve-thirteen train. On one occasion William Jennings Bryan, three-time Democratic presidential candidate, got off the train to stretch his legs and thought the whole town had turned out to see him. "He didn't know that the town always turned out for the Sunday twelve-thirteen" laughed Mrs. Massa (Delozier 5).

Young people would hang out at the depot. It was a good place for courting couples to meet each other. At night, teenage boys would gather together and talk around the stove.

A very important impact of the railroad was the cultural and educational opportunities it made possible. "We were cut off from everything," Dottie Williams recalled. She added, "If we had not had the Tennessee Central, we would not have had Tennessee Polytechnic Institute, which brought many cultured people here." In 1916, crowds of people would meet the students and hotels sent wagons to pick up the students and their luggage.

From this time to the late 1920s was the heyday for the railroads. At one time there were six passenger trains and two freight trains running in Cookeville every day. The stockmarket crash of 1929 diminished the demand for train service dramatically. "Many people lost their jobs, and hobos were a common sight in the boxcars of the T. C." recalls Earl Wallace (Wallace 8).

The Second World War breathed life back into the railroads in 1941. The trains carried German and Italian prisoners to a detention camp outside of Crossville. The trains also carried soldiers to their destinations. "We girls waved to the soldiers as I'm sure girls did all over the world," writes Gene Evelyn Warren (Wallace 7). But by the end of the war, the demand for passenger trains had declined.

The reason for the decline was the new Interstate Highway 40 and the completion of Highway 70, the availability of cheaper automobiles, and the opening of several transport company terminals in Cookeville. Also, Greyhound buslines began running from Nashville to Knoxville. The T. C. could not compete with the cars, buses, and trucks: "On July 31, 1955, the last passenger train ran between Nashville and Emory Gap" (Wallace 9).

Freight service continued until 1968. John Lusk, a freight conductor, put a wreath of flowers on the front of his train for its final two-weeks' run. "The saddest thing in the world was when it closed" Mrs. Dottie Williams remembers (Wallace 8). It was the end of an era for our community and for many other communities all across America. All the depots in the county except Cookeville have been razed. The railroad has changed hands many times, and today is owned by the Nashville and Eastern railroad authority.

"Though trains no longer stop at the Cookeville depot, it continues to remind visitors of the heyday of trains and of the railroad's importance in the history of Putnam County" (Wallace 10). In April 1984, "Friends of the Depot" was born. "Friends of the Depot" is a group of concerned citizens working together to keep the spirit of the railroad alive for future generations. Their work involves restoring, fixing, and preserving the depot and railroad memorabilia.

The Friends of the Depot have begun to reap the rewards of their hard work and dedication. In 1984, The United States Department of the Interior listed the Cookeville Depot in the National Register of Historic Places. Quite an honor for such a small and modest structure! It is now a museum.

The Putnam County Chamber of Commerce has also been instrumental in keeping our "railroad heritage" alive. On April 25-26 a passenger train will carry people from Cookeville to Buffalo Valley and back again. This event will be called the Cookeville Dogwood Flyer Train (Foy 1). This is truly a momentous occasion for the people of this area! It will mark the first time in forty years that a train has carried passengers up or down Silver Point Hill.

"It has taken ten years of hard work to bring the train back to the mountain and the railroad is doing good here again," states Chamber of Commerce CEO Eldon Leslie (Foy 1). The railway has been improved and can once again carry passengers as well as freight. Because of these improvements, we may see more and more of the passenger train trips to various places in the area. "In these ways a part of our Upper Cumberland heritage is being preserved for future generations and shared with the present one" (Wallace 10).

Works Cited

Delozier, Mary Jean. "The Railroad Arrived 100 Years Ago," *Highballer*.
    Cookeville: Friends of the Depot, 1990.

Foy, Don. "Dogwood Flyer," *(Cookeville) Herald Citizen*, March 30, 1997.

McMillan, Bob. "Depot Links Present to Past," *(Cookeville) Herald Citizen,*
    April 24, 1985.

_____ "Trains Arrive Here in 1890," *(Cookeville) Herald Citizen*, April 21, 1985.

Wallace, Connie. *Railroading in Putnam County.* Cookeville, TN:
    Cookeville Depot Museum, 1987.

-Tennessee Technical Institute
Heidemarie Wiedner, Instructor

Why Aren't There More Female Computer Scientists?

Wanda Husted

"The demographics of this country are such that the United States will not have enough engineers and scientists unless underrepresented groups increase their participation (Spertus 1). This is complicated by the fact that the percentage of female computer science students is increasing at a very slow rate and may even be decreasing. Over forty-nine percent of all professionals in the workforce are female, yet females only comprise about thirty percent of employed computer scientists (Frenkel 2). Several studies have been done in an effort to determine the cause of this disparity. After all, "There is no reason why women should not make up half the labor force in computing...It's not as if computing involved lifting 125 pound weights" (Frenkel 3). The researchers have concluded that stereotyping plays a definitive role in discouraging women from moving into Computer Science. While it may seem surprising to discover that stereotyping is still prevalent in the enlightened nineties, it is nevertheless a fact. Professional women in Computer Science often suffer from the ill-effects of stereotyping. Stereotyping against women is first encountered in the common use of sex-biased software. A female's education is also colored by stereotyping which sometimes begins as early as preschool and continues through college. Finally, women also encounter the infamous "glass ceiling" as they climb the corporate ladder.

Women first suffer from the effects of stereotyping as they use sex-biased software. Charles Huff and Joel Cooper did research to find out why the computer "is more alluring to boys than it is to girls." According to their results, when software is designed specifically for girls, designers usually generate learning tools, whereas games are usually generated when software is designed for boys. When designing for the generic "student," games are usually the end result. This research suggests that "Programs written for students are written…with boys in mind." Huff and Cooper conclude that "It is not the computer, or even the software, that is at the root of the sex bias in software, but the expectations and stereotypes of the designers of the software" (532). In another study, Sara Keissler found that men also dominated the covers of computer games. Upon examining the covers of computer games 28 men and 4 women were illustrated. On one cover, two women were playing Monopoly with two men, on another, a woman was depicted as a "very fat queen," and on the last cover there appeared a "princess in supplicating position on the floor" (157).

Women are also discriminated against at the college level. Henry Etzkowitz studied students at a leading research university and discovered a "sexual separation of scientists" (Frenkel 8). He found that certain areas of science are labeled as male or female disciplines, which leads each gender to avoid certain areas. Computer science theory and particle physics are pretty much "off limits" to women, whereas some male faculty consider natural language to be better for females. This is because natural language is closer to the traditional gender roles such as the "expressive role and typing skills in software." In "The Classroom Climate: Chilly for Women?" Bernice R. Sandler made several observations which indicate that both men and women are guilty of stereotyping: females are interrupted more than males; faculty members make eye contact with male students more often than with female students; faculty members are more likely to know and use the names of their male students rather than the names of their female students; and females are often asked fewer or easier questions than males. Sandler writes, "Singly, these behaviors probably have little effect. However, when they occur repeatedly they give a powerful message to women: they are not as worthwhile as men nor are they expected to participate fully in class, in college, or in life at large" (149).

Because of stereotyping, rising above the glass ceiling in corporate America is hard for women. This is due, in part, to the fact the "most of management is male and feels more comfortable dealing with other men" (Drakos). However, female behavior does not receive the same acceptance as does equivalent behavior exhibited by men. Sandler wrote "He is 'assertive'; she is 'aggressive' or 'hostile.' He 'lost his cool,' implying it was an aberration; she's 'emotional' or 'menopausal.' Thus, her behavior is devalued; even when it is the same as his" (151). Women are often overlooked for promotions or raised because of this "negative" behavior, which keeps them in the lower echelons at large companies. An independent study reported in *Business Week* said that "while women started out with comparable pay, within 10 years they were 25% behind their male counterparts (Frenkel 4).

As the research cited above indicated, software is generally developed for a male audience, thus locking in the inequities of the past. This type of stereotyping, coupled with the discrimination women face during their education, sets the stage for male dominance in the field of computer science and results in lower pay for women in the field. Professional women in Computer Science often suffer from the ill-effects of stereotyping. Fortunately discrimination against women has decreased significantly since the turn of the century. However, as the researchers have shown, stereotyping still plays a detrimental role in software, schooling, and the professional careers of women.

Works Cited

Huff, Charles and Joel Cooper. "Sex Bias in Educational Software: The Effect of Designer's Stereotypes on the Software They Design," *Journal of Applied Social Psychology*, 17.6 (1987): 519-532.

Drakos, Nikos. "The Glass Ceiling," Translation initiated by ellens @ai.mit.edu., April 6, 1994. Online. Internet. 17 Feb 1997. Available WWW: http://www.ai.mit.edu/people/ellens/Gende...star3_2_8.html #SECTION0002800000000000000

Etzkowitz, associate professor of Sociology at SUNY Purchase, and visiting scientist, Department of Computer Science, Columbia University. Unpublished. Workshop presentation: "The Power of Paradigms" 1990.

Frenkel, Karen, A. "Women and Computing," *Communictions of the ACM*, (November 1990): full text. Online. Internet. 17 February 1997. AvailableWWW: http://www.cpsr..org/cpse/gender/frenkel.cacm.womcomp.

Husted, Robert W. Peer Editor. Husband to the author of this paper. 19 February, 1997, 2 hours.

Kiesler, Sara; Sproull, Lee; and Eccles, Jacquelynne. "Pool Halls, Chips and War Games: Women in the Culture of Computing," *Psychology of Women Quarterly*, Vol. 9, (1985): 451-562.

Sandler, Bernice R. "The Classroom Climate: Chilly for Women?" *The Academic Handbook*, (1988): 146-152.

Spertus, Ellen. "Why Are There So Few Female Computer Scientists?" (1991): full text. Online. Internet. 17 Feb 1997. Available WWW: www:http/snyside.sunnyside.com/cpsr/gender/Spertus_womcs.txt.

-De Anza College
John Swensson

III

Writing to Argue a Position

Like writing to inform and explain, argumentative and persuasive writing can rely primarily on personal experience, outside reading and research, or a combination of both. The difference is that the purpose of argumentative writing is always to take a stand on an issue or topic about which there is some difference of opinion. The topic may be a highly controversial social or political issue, a less well-publicized issue of whose importance a writer wishes to convince his or her readers, or a generally held view or interpretation that the writer wishes to convince his or her readers to see in a new light. Sometimes the writer's purpose is to try to change readers' minds; sometimes it is to convince readers to be more open to seeing the subject in a new light; at other times the purpose may actually be to move readers further, to convince them to take action in order to improve some existing condition. The essays in this chapter suggest the wide range of possibilities available when writing to argue a position.

In "The Haitian Exodus" Robert Lee Goudy, who served with the Coast Guard patrolling the Caribbean for Haitian boat people bound illegally for the United States, uses his personal experience to try to persuade readers to see the plight of the Haitians in a more sympathetic light. Tia Collins, in "Making a Connection," focuses on what she calls a "fracture in the American family structure," identifying what she sees as the main causes of this fracture and offering her views about what parents should do to help connect family members again. In "Can't Say No, If You Don't Know," Margaret Cooney argues that the drug Rohypnol—the notorious "love drug" that has been used to incapacitate women in a number of cases of date rape—should be banned in the United States; further she urges readers to boycott the company that produces the drug. In "Love vs. Hate and Fear," Marit Brickman tries to convince readers to come to a more sympathetic view of homosexuals, arguing that "anything short of equal rights, privileges, and responsibilities for all human beings is, by logical deduction, discrimination"; recognizing resistance to her position, Brickman acknowledges opposing arguments and attempts to refute them.

Cyndi Dickey uses a different kind of strategy in "No Time for Cloning Around," her argument against the cloning of human beings: Pushing the possibility to its extreme, she suggests that too little is known about the kind of beings that would result from cloning to risk peopling the world with clones. In "Arctic National Wildlife Refuge," Jackie Franze uses her extensive research to make the case that oil drilling should be prohibited within the reserve, "one of the largest wildlife sanctuaries in the world"; in her argument Franze presents three main arguments for those in favor of such drilling and offers her specific refutations for each case.

Finally, the chapter ends with two essays that argue opposing sides on the same controversial subject: the teaching of Ebonics, or Black English, in public schools—an issue that received considerable media attention in 1997 when the Oakland, California, school declared Ebonics a legitimate separate language and instituted policies to train teachers in its use. In "The Ebonics Issue: It's Easier to Understand When It's in Black and White," Tobias Sherwood argues against teaching Ebonics as a separate language, offering his evidence that it is a dialect of English, and then lays out a proposal for a significantly scaled-back program for helping students who speak Black English. Ginger Evans, on the other hand, argues in "Ebonics: The Whole Truth" that while the Oakland board may have been mistaken in requesting federal funding to treat Black English as a second language, the evidence of its speakers' problems in school is such that radical measures do need to be taken.

The essays in this chapter suggest the many challenges of writing to argue a position, as well as the strategies available to student writers in meeting such challenges. In evaluating the strength of each argument, read with an open mind and close attention to the quality of evidence presented.

The Haitian Exodus
Robert Lee Goudy
(Maysville, Pennsylvania)

I can see the boats in the distance, headed out to sea again. The Haitians always do this, set sail when they see us sitting out here on our Coast Guard ships. They believe that we will take them to the United States; but they are actually going to be taken back to Port-au-Prince, Haiti. We will burn their rickety, homebuilt boats and then head back to our station, ten miles off the coast of Haiti in the Windward Passage.

I participated in this series of actions over and over while I served aboard the U. S. Coast Guard Cutter Bear, five years ago.

When I enlisted in the Coast Guard, I thought that I would be helping to prevent illegal aliens from entering the United States. In fact, however, we were there to prevent the Haitians from an assured death at sea; there is less than a one percent chance of making the 120 mile voyage from Haiti to the United States through the Windward Passage, the most violent body of water in the Caribbean Sea. I also had a problem with the Haitians personally. Why don't they stay in their own country? Why come to my country? I really didn't understand them at all, even to the point of holding a resentment toward them. I felt this way right from the beginning, even before I enlisted.

Everything changed for me, however, in the summer of 1991 during my first Alien Migration Interdiction Operation. This was when I first met a Haitian immigrant.

It was my turn to assume the duty as small boat engineer, and armed with an M16 I felt tough: No Haitian would think twice about messing with me. I already knew about Haiti—the overpopulation, the famine, the rampant diseases that ravaged its people: cholera, dysentery, AIDs. The children have a 30 percent chance of dying before they reach adulthood. These were simply trivial facts to me; I had a duty to perform.

I saw the simple wooden sailboats as we approached. The boats measuring about twenty to thirty feet in length, were built from two-by-fours and scraps torn from buildings. They were overloaded with an average of seventy-five people, all yelling about going to America. As we drew close to the first boat, I found myself wondering what would drive so many people to such extreme measures to "invade" my country. Then we started to load these people on our smallboats and transfer them to the ship. There were hundreds of people, all of them emaciated and sick. They were pitiful, having no personal possessions and being too weak to climb the ladder up to the ship. When we approached their boats, they would get so excited trying to climb into our smallboats that they would capsize their own. These were the people we were defending our country from? And with guns?

The first person I pulled into the boat was a young woman. She was soaked, as were all of the Haitians, wearing some tattered rags, and she looked weak and worn down. But when I looked into her eyes, I saw a brilliance and clarity that told me she thought she was going to America. I, however, knew her true destination. By nightfall we had to leave our patrol area to offload the 450 Haitians we had intercepted that day. Being on a 270-foot ship, we were dangerously overloaded. We had no food or facilities to support all the Haitians: so many people, and there were five other Coast Guard ships still picking up more.

On that first night, as we headed into Port-au-Prince, I realized what I had failed to see previously. The Haitians were a people with absolutely nothing except what they wore and each other. They simply wanted a chance to live, instead of the grim existence they had on Haiti. This was a chance that they would never have at home, so they would risk everything, including their lives and their children, to journey to America, to have the same chances that I have had. That night the Haitian people earned an enormous amount of respect from me and at the same time made me question my beliefs. Who are we to determine the fate of these people? Why shouldn't they have the same chances that we have? Have we forgotten that the United States is a country of immigrants?

-Harrisonburg Area Community College
Cathryn Amadahl, Instructor

Making a Connection
Tia Collins

A fracture in the American family structure today lies in the discontinuity between the generations. Due to the fast-paced lives Americans lead, the lack of emphasis on family history, and the separation of families, communication has been severed from family life.

The fast pace of American life is causing people to shift their priorities. We live in a society where money and power take precedence over the establishment of family values. Barry Levinson depicts this in his movie, *Avalon*. Here, one son, Jules, rejects family tradition because he is so caught up in trying to make money. The focus of most parents today is on the provision of material possessions they did not have as children themselves. If children today are not wearing the "in" brand of jeans, driving an expensive car, and living in a big, pretty house, then both parents and children feel devalued. The focus is on the outer structure, not the inner structure. The main priorities should be on the inner structure of the family, not what the family presents to the world. Putting forth effort to keep up a facade, families lose the energy to instill values in their children.

The lack of emphasis on family history also creates a lack of communication in families. Family history serves to connect us to one another. It serves as a vehicle to self-discovery, adding texture to our lives. We base choices, values, and morals on such knowledge. Through knowledge or their heritage, people become proud. In turn, their children become proud. People are able to become strong in the face of adversity by knowing someone else in the family could overcome such trials. By listening to elders' stories, children know where to turn in times of confusion and need. In *Avalon*, what Sam, the father, is trying to accomplish by retelling family history is realized though his son Michael. When Michael goes to see Sam in the nursing home,

60

Sam's age does not allow his memory to serve him, but Michael remembers and passes the story along to his own son. A connection is made and values are passed from one generation to the next. Of course, all aspects of family history are not pleasant. Why is it still important to know of family history? People need to learn the source of the problems so as to correct them. People have a hard time delving into themselves to find answers as to why they do the things they do. This may have something to do with being frightened of finding out that the problem was passed down through generations in the family, thus having a reason to be ashamed of family. If this is the case, then some importance of family structure is important to them, and undoing what's been done by taking a stand for future generations is a must.

The separation of families, immediate and extended alike, also breaks down the coherence of the family. Many people are concerned with themselves and their own struggles and advances in society. They're barely concerned with their immediate families, let alone the family in its entirety. In *Avalon*, the breakdown of the family occurs gradually as the families move from Avalon, an apartment building, to row houses, and finally, to the suburbs. To go even further, Sam ends up in a nursing home completely alone. The connections between family members lessen as the space between them increases. As the family members fall away, so do the traditions once important to them. Each family member's commitment to participation is required to make a family complete. The separation of family results in a loss of values.

One of the main reasons for the separation among immediate family members is television, ironically one of the material possessions people work so hard to attain. Televisions have invaded family space. In some cases, the actors or characters substitute as quasi-parents for children. By dominating the time they spend together, television breaks down the relationship between parent and child and between parent and parent. When family activities and rituals are neglected, so is the communication essential to human development. Communication not only improves understanding between family members, but of people outside the family as well. Because of the one-sided relationship with television characters, children grow up not knowing how to communicate with others. Bringing family rituals back into daily life can help to connect family members and improve communication between them. E. B. White's essay "Once More to the Lake" points out the importance of such rituals for giving a father a better understanding of his child and himself and for giving a son a more meaningful perspective of life than if he just were only to live vicariously through characters on television. People need to take their children on family outings; they will look back on them just as E. B. White did—and cherish them.

Children need the structure of close-knit families whose members truly care about one another's well-being. Such children will grow up to be conscious of the needs society has as a whole; they will rarely end up adding to the corruption of our culture. In order to make this connection, church, family discussion time, and storytelling must be priorities in the home. First, church must not be something that's only thought about on Sunday. The values and lessons taught there must be integrated into the home on a daily basis. Parents need to make sure children understand why it's so important to pray and read the word of God. Next, openness in family discussion is essential to being a close-knit family. Parents must not have narrow minds, but should welcome discussions about what goes on in children's lives today. Things do change; younger generations will face confrontations that previous generations never dreamed of. But through the connection of generations, they will be able to come to their parents asking for help in decision-making, whether it be about smoking a cigarette or smoking marijuana. Finally, storytelling time can be set aside for either telling family history, reading short stories, taking children to the library, or having time for question and answers regarding their own personal readings. Through reading, children are better able to get to know themselves as individuals. It is by sharing these activities that families express themselves, thus improving relationships, bettering the development of the children, and staying connected.

-Tulsa Community College
Judy Burnham, Instructor

Can't Say No, If You Don't Know

Margaret F. Cooney
(South Fork, Pennsylvania)

A little white tablet, Rohypnol, has gained notoriety as the "love drug" of the 1990s. Called "roofies," ruffies," "roche," R-2," "rib," "rope," or "rophy," these tasteless and odorless pills can be furtively slipped into any beverage where they quickly dissolve. Within a few short minutes, this potent substance renders the unsuspecting victim dizzy and disoriented. The consumer experiences difficulty moving her arms and legs, and eventually passes out with little or no memory of what happened. The drug—legally produced and prescribed elsewhere, particularly in Europe and South America—is used to treat insomnia and as a preanesthesia agent. However, importation into the United States was banned earlier this year. According to Jim Tolliver of the

Drug Enforcement Agency, "The government is concerned with four popular misuses of Rohypnol: when taken with alcohol, when taken with heroin and cocaine, when taken alone, and when taken in date rape situations." Because the potential abuse of this drug far outweighs any legitimate medical use, production should be halted. There is no reason for Rohypnol to exist.

Flunitrazepan (brand name Rohypnol) is a powerful tranquilizer, similar to Valium, but ten times stronger. Rohypnol rapidly produces a sedative effect, temporary amnesia, muscle relaxation, and a slowing of psychomotor responses within fifteen to twenty minutes after oral administration. Rohypnol is sometimes referred to as the "forget pill" because when a person wakes up, she can't remember. "Roofie rape" becomes the perfect crime; the perpetrator doesn't have to worry about a witness. Rapists wrongly reason they have not done anything wrong. After all, the woman did not refuse. Their misguided consciences are salved. "Roofies" have appeared on campuses throughout the United States. There is strong evidence that their ingestion led to at least ten date rape situations at Penn State University this year according to the Penn State Collegian.

Women are not the sole victims of this drug. Businessmen awake to find their money, jewelry, and credit cards missing. Gay men are strongly advised never to accept an opened drink, especially from a stranger. As insidious and perilous as this may sound, the dangers of the drug don't stop here. Rohypnol, taken alone as a primary intoxicant, appeals to schoolchildren and those on a limited budget who are looking for a "buzz." Cheaper than alcohol (street value from $1 to $5), "roche" causes no problems with blood alcohol levels. Only an expensive urine test will detect its presence; therefore, it is highly unlikely that a user will be arrested for substance abuse. On the other hand, ingesting the drug, while alcohol is in the system, can put someone in a coma. Rohypnol is touted as a "parachute" or remedy for depression that follows a stimulant high by allaying withdrawal symptoms in a state of oblivion. Addicts utilize Rohypnol as an enhancer for low-quality heroin and in combination with cocaine to moderate the effects of binges.

Naturally, any illegal use of Rohypnol should be a concern; however, it is reprehensible that it is given to innocent participants in the hope of lowering inhibitions and facilitating conquest. In response to pressure to have the sedative reclassified as a dangerous drug, the maker of the "date rape pill" announced an ad campaign to fight its abuse. The Swiss-based pharmaceutical manufacturer, Hoffman-LaRoche & Co., plans to produce radio and television public service announcements warning women to be cautious in bars. Conversely, Hoffman-LaRoche & Co. fears that education will worsen the problem. The company ironically contends that after hearing about the pill's potential, everyone will seek it out. So why is it still made?

In Germany, Hoffman-LaRoche & Co. removed the drug from retail distribution, restricting it to hospital use only. In America, Rohypnol is not recognized as an acceptable medication; there are safer alternatives. So why is it still made?

Sadly the answer appears to be purely greed. Some companies, even highly respectable ones, refuse to turn away from easy money.

Since Rohypnol is a dangerous drug that is being introduced and "pushed" in our country, citizens should demand protection by having the United States government pressure Hoffman-LaRoche & Co. to halt its production. How could this be accomplished? By refusing to purchase any pharmaceuticals from this company, a serious statement would be made. A drastic step, but in this case a necessary one to stop the victimization of innocent people. After all, you can't say no, if you don't know.

-Penn State, Altoona Campus
Sandra Petrulionis, Instructor

Love vs. Hate and Fear
Marit Brickman
(Mill Valley, California)

Brenda, 19, was run down by a car in Minnesota yesterday. It was not an accident. Nick, 57, was stabbed 15 times and died in a hospital in Florida last week. Nancy, 36, was beaten up on her way home in Oregon last Tuesday.

These crimes against gays and lesbians happen daily. As a matter of fact, an estimated 7,500 hate crimes based on sexual orientation are committed each year in the United States.

Most people are appalled by these atrocities, yet when the discussion turns to the establishment of equal rights for gays and lesbians, sentiments change. In other words, discrimination against gays and lesbians is on a sliding scale. A person might find a criminal act unacceptable, but believe that neutral or positive literature about gays and lesbians should be removed from all public libraries. Another individual might believe gays and lesbians should be allowed to register as domestic partners, but oppose a priest sanctifying that union through marriage.

In my view, discrimination is discrimination. Anything short of equal rights, privileges, and responsibilities for all human beings is, by logical deduction, discrimination. What is interesting to me is that people who do not share my view on equal rights for lesbians and gays justify their discrimination in an array of issues. I will take a closer look at these issues below.

Let's first consider gay marriage, a hotly debated topic. People who oppose gay marriage argue that it is against God's will and that it threatens "traditional family values." I am intrigued when people, without God's consent, use God as a silent partner to collaborate their views. The Bible makes six references to homosexuality. These Biblical references are not conclusive on whether homosexuality is right or wrong. In fact, religious scholars cannot agree on an interpretation. As a layperson, I will not make a judgment on this issue, but my understanding is that God sent Jesus to preach God's will on this earth 2000 years ago. Jesus never made any judgment against homosexuality or homosexuals. His message centered on love, community, and respect for all human beings. If we are all created equal and in the mirror of God, is not our sexuality and sexual preference one of God's creations?

I find the argument that gays and lesbians threaten "traditional family values" the most engaging and amusing. "Traditional family values" are defined as a heterosexual, married couple with or without children. How can gays and lesbians pose a threat to someone else's family? Gays and lesbians do not contend they want to strip away other people's rights. They have not said that their choice is better than someone else's. Frankly speaking, I don't know what is so attractive about so-called traditional family values considering that 50 percent of all heterosexual marriages end in divorce, and an appalling percentage are characterized by domestic violence or child abuse.

Another argument used against granting gays and lesbians equal rights involves children. This is perhaps the most emotionally charged issue for both sides of the debate and it is certainly the issue on which the opposition attracts the largest following. The main argument is that children of gay and lesbian parents will be harassed, especially in school, and that this is not fair to the children. In addition, opponents of equal rights for lesbians and gays often contend that the children themselves will grow up to become gays or lesbians. Interestingly enough, the people who argue that children of gay and lesbian parents will be teased are the same people that will not allow any neutral or positive information or books about gays and lesbians in the school libraries. They will not allow teachers to educate youth on the fact that different sexual orientations exist. They seek to prevent gays and lesbians and their friends from meeting in school clubs to discuss different issues concerning sexual orientation. So how do they expect to make room for understanding and acceptance when they seek to put a lid on anything that can prevent harassment in the first place?

The argument that children raised by gays and lesbians will themselves become gay or lesbian is not supported by research. On the contrary, the research that has been done shows no correlation between how a child is raised and that child's sexual orientation. Research has shown, however, that human sexual orientation may be determined in our genes before birth, although this research is inconclusive. What I find interesting is that siblings often have the same sexual orientation—homosexual or heterosexual—which supports the theory and preliminary research findings of biological determination. For the sake of this argument, let's say that children who are raised by lesbian and gay parents grow up to be lesbian or gay—what is wrong with that? Isn't determining this to be undesirable implying that being heterosexual is superior—and therefore discriminatory in itself?

Where does this lead us? Probably right back to where we started. My arguments will probably not sway many people. But why is that? Why is it that logic often works slowly, if at all, when we discuss discrimination? I believe it is because people's fear of gays and lesbians, or any minority, lies deeper in human make-up than the thinking brain.

The famous psychologist Maslow used his needs hierarchy to show that being human is to strive to gain acceptance from fellow humans and to seek to fulfill individual potential. Even if we are the most intelligent creatures on this planet, on a very basic level we behave like most other creatures in competing for food and shelter. On a more complex level, we also strive for group acceptance and self-realization. Just as in the animal world, it is apt to refer to this struggle as "the survival of the fittest."

I believe therefore, that we try to protect ourselves, our values, and our belongings from anything that can threaten the safety of our life or lifestyle. As such, I think that minorities are seen as threatening—they will take our jobs, our neighborhoods, and other things of "ours." Whatever the threat, our first instinct is to protect ourselves. In light of this, it is perhaps natural that heterosexuals initially try to prevent lesbians and gays from gaining access to what they see as their privileges. But—and there is a big *but*—such fears can be combated with information, education, and communication. Consequently, the treatment of lesbians and gays has improved as people realize that lesbians and gays do not diminish the lives of heterosexuals.

I believe a lot of people understand that lesbians and gays do not threaten their existence, so why is it that some people, educated and informed, continue to oppress this particular group? Why is it that some people seem to find pleasure in inflicting pain on others or accept than pain is inflicted? My best try at answering this question, to which only God holds the answer, is to submit the proposition that a Dr. Jekyll and Mr. Hyde lives inside of each of us. Humans seem to be drawn toward experiencing the extremes of life and we all operate on a scale between, for example, light and dark, pleasure and pain, order and chaos, love and hate. As painful as this can make our lives, it also makes life interesting and challenging. But I believe it is possible to experience these extremes without inflicting pain on others. We all have to find a balance and weigh the impact of our behavior when "we take a walk on the wild side." I believe Robin Hood found that balance, while Adolph Hitler did not.

Hate and fear seem to be so readily available to our world, while love and understanding seem to have drawn the shorter straw. Ask any lesbian or gay person. It is not possible to have too much love, commitment, and extended community in this world which, after all, is the only "threat" in accepting lesbians and gays. It is time for us to have the courage to stop the hate, to demand equal rights for lesbians and gays, and to move on to more challenging and pressing matters in this world.

-University of San Francisco
Barbara Moran, Instructor

No Time For Cloning Around

Cyndi Dickey
(Little Elm, Texas)

A certain arrogant element of humanity regards itself as the most superior of life forms in the universe and has dominated everything and everyone in its path since the beginning of time. Evidence of such bigots' self-centeredness is reflected throughout history, revealed by decisions made in favor of their own progress regardless of the adverse impact these may have on other life forms. Destruction of animal species, ecological systems, and less aggressive races of people has frequently been perpetrated by intellects who consider their own interests and progress as being more relevant than anyone or anything else's. To add to the frustration of this reality, these "masterminds" also have had the slickest way of convincing their prey that whatever it is they are about to propose will be for the betterment of the victim. They also rationalize that their own grandiose ideas are a result of the evolution of the human mind—something which they ignorantly think everyone both believes and values.

What then, is the newest proposal set forth by these forward-thinking scientists on the twenty-first century's horizon? Perpetuate conceitedness— try cloning human beings.

Now, at first, the average citizen might not regard cloning, particularly of animals, as a problem at all. After all, if cattle, sheep, pigs, fish, chickens, and turkeys could be cloned, the worldwide starvation issue would be greatly lessened, if not completely eradicated. Greater numbers of animals could be created in greater quantities since some animals' inability to conceive would no longer impede the consideration of each animal from producing offspring. Also, because the genes of the animal could be manipulated by the one doing the cloning, diseases in the animal could be sifted out, as well as the animal's propensity towards storing fat. The result could mean that the quality of meat supplied through such a venture could be better for human consumption than ever before, especially if the one doing the manipulating is truly looking out for the good of mankind. This, of course, leads to the greatest question when considering the application of cloning human beings: Is the underlying motive for cloning as pure as it may seem?

What would happen if scientists cloned a human being? What characteristics would be noted as the most desirable ones to put into the clone, and who should get to make that decision? Giving clones slimmer bodies and the lack of a gene which adds to greater likelihood of heart disease or cancer might make the clone live a long time, but will a long life for a clone be good if its value system decides that killing off real human beings is okay? Or, will the clone even have a value system? What will people do with a clone once it is brought into existence, only to find that it lacks a conscience and a soul? Will people then be forced with the decision of having to kill the living being, which would then serve to compromise the value system of the one having to do the killing? If people are confused about aborting their own human children out of their own wombs, how much more so will they be confused if confronted with the choice of whether to let a clone live or die? As far as the legal system goes, jails are already frequently overcrowded with delinquent human beings. If conscienceless clones were not destroyed, they would probably have to live out their very long lives in prisons at the expense of the human beings who so foolishly brought them into the world.

Just suppose clones are brought into existence that are better looking, healthier, and smarter than the people who encouraged their creation in the first place. Will humans want to hang around with them? Although it is a known fact that people like to spend time with individuals who are talented and interesting, they also do not like to be compared with those who appear superior; such a dilemma would seem to add to the very issue of racism which the government, social organizations, and many individuals are already trying so hard to deal with.

Also, how would it be to have to physically and mentally compete with clones? A human's best efforts would be like child's play to a clone who would have every genetic advantage, not to mention the absence of degenerative, inherited disease factors. Would human beings be able to keep their coveted pro-sports positions, professional acting careers, beauty-queen titles, business executive roles, teaching positions, or, dare I say it, scientific professions? Or, would clones edge the human race out of every endeavor that they had previously accomplished, and if so, what then would the human race do for employment? Then, too, if insurance companies are already trying to find reasons not to have to cover an individual who has the potential for diseases, how much more will they be able to rationalize not having to cover the human being in the future—especially, if the one making the decision, in actuality, is a clone itself?!

All in all, although some may argue that the enlightened scientists of today are brewing up a plan which could jettison the evolving human mind into a positive future through the use of cloning, I believe that such matters are too vast for the human mind to comprehend and put the very idea of it in the same category as the atomic bomb's use in warfare. Knowledge of anything, no matter how reasonable or just it may seem, can only remain so in the hands of someone completely reliable, and what human being can lay absolute claim to that?

-Collin County Community College
Sherill Cobb, Instructor

Arctic National Wildlife Refuge
Jackie Franze
(Fort Wayne, Indiana)

The Arctic National Wildlife Refuge (ANWR) is one of the largest wildlife sanctuaries in the world. It is located in the northeastern section of the state of Alaska on the edge of the Arctic Ocean. The refuge consists of approximately 19 million acres of tundra, hills, rivers, and streams. It is bountiful in its diverse wildlife ("The Arctic National Wildlife Refuge"; Speer 42).

To environmentalists, this refuge is considered to be "the treasure" of North America. ANWR is also treasured by others for different reasons. It is believed to contain substantial amounts of oil. Oil drilling in ANWR versus preserving ANWR is a very complex and controversial issue. Preserving the pristine environment of ANWR is more valuable than any amount of oil that could be obtained from it.

Energy Security

The oil industry wants us to believe that drilling in ANWR would provide us with energy security. We would not be dependent on foreign oil, and our energy needs would not be subjected to the political upheavals in foreign countries. If U. S. energy security relies on this oil, then why are we selling our Prudhoe Bay oil to Japan and other foreign countries? It is now being traded on world markets. This is increasing the profits of the oil companies. This isn't energy security; it's outright greed.

It is also being debated how much oil is actually recoverable in ANWR. Lisa Speer, a senior project scientist at the Natural Resources Defense Council, reports that estimates by the U. S. Interior Department state only 3.2 billion barrels of oil could be taken from these oil fields. This is barely enough to fuel the U. S. for six months (43). Oil drilling in ANWR is not going to solve the long-term energy needs of this country.

Safety

Dealing with safe extraction and transportation of oil gives rise to several issues. Alyeska, the conglomerate of seven oil companies operating in Alaska, promised when the 800-mile pipeline between Prudhoe Bay and the port of Valdez was built that every measure possible would be taken to preserve the environment. State-of-the-art pollution technology and a written contingency plan detailed precisely how an accident would be handled and what equipment would be used.

Facts however, prove that Alyeska has a total disregard for the environment. Tami Thomas, a member of Alyeska's oil response team working in Valdez states, "We'd have spills daily. We'd put a boom around a tanker…,but our supervisors didn't want us to pick up the oil. They'd order the boom opened to let another ship in" (Davidson 82). Dan Lawn is the Department of Environmental Conservation's representative in Valdez. He observed that ballast water was being dumped into the port of Valdez without being treated first. Ballast water is water containing oil residues carried in empty cargo tanks for tanker stability. To clean oil sludge from terminals, approved biodegradable detergents were axed in favor of toxic unapproved detergents. Lawn also states that Alyeska disconnected equipment from their oil storage tanks that burned off toxic vapors. Next, they cut personnel on their oil response teams (Davidson 83).

Repeatedly, Alyeska was told their spill contingency plan was inadequate. There were not enough booms, skimmers, or dispersants available. They consistently failed to correct these problems. They said it wasn't cost effective. In his book, *In the Wake of the Exxon Valdez*, author Art Davidson writes that in 1984, the Environmental Protection Agency (EPA) concluded that Alyeska was not prepared for an oil spill (87). What happened to the promise that Alyeska had made to protect the environment? It was a lie. Alyeska had no intention of protecting the environment.

The result was a catastrophic oil spill in March 1989. The Exxon Valdez ran aground on Bligh Reef spilling 11,000,000 gallons of oil into Prince William Sound. Alyeska was totally unprepared. For almost three days, they did nothing. They tried to organize a spill response from scratch. There was not enough equipment or manpower to fight the spill. Precious time was lost arguing about what to do. All the while, the Exxon Valdez sat hemorrhaging its cargo of oil (Lewis 5-7).

The damage was intense. The animal populations were desecrated. The fishing season was destroyed. Dr. Zach Willey reports that over twenty tons of dead animals were picked up (1). How many more went off to die alone in agony? Today, Prince William Sound has not recovered. Rick Steiner, a marine biologist and fisherman living near the sound, has studied the aftermath of the disaster. He asserts that even though the oil slick is gone, many beaches still have patches of tar-like oil. Numbers of birds and wildlife are down dramatically from their pre-spill status. In describing the scope of the spill he states, "The oil spread over some 10,000 square miles and oiled more than 1,200 miles of coastline—including shores of three national parks, three national wildlife refuges and a national forest" (6). Is this what the oil industry considers preserving a safe environment? Many of the thousands of lawsuits filed against Exxon by the U. S. Government, the state of Alaska, fishermen, and environmental groups have yet to be settled by the court system.

The oil tankers themselves also raise serious safety concerns. In his article, "America's Oil Tanker Mess," Abe Dane raises several issues. Twenty years ago, the oil tankers were 600 feet long and had a capacity for oil cargo of 30,000 tons. Today, the tankers are 1,200 feet long and are able to carry 500,000 tons. Tankers have become twice as long, but are capable of carrying sixteen times the load. The reason for this is less steel. Today's modern tankers are one part steel to six parts oil. Dane points out, "The low ratio of steel to cargo…makes them vulnerable to rupture at the gentlest brush with an unyielding object" (52). Why would an oil industry, that is supposedly so concerned with safety, build ships like this? It is just another example of greed.

In 1990, the U. S. Congress passed the Oil Pollution Act. One of the provisions is that all new tankers constructed for use in U. S. waters have a double hull by 1994, and all single hull tankers will be banned by the year 2010. The oil industry is pouring millions of dollars into fighting this regulation. They say they can't possible meet this time frame. It isn't cost effective.

In Exxon's annual report for 1995, it states the company's net profit as $6.5 billion. Just one year's profit was $6.5 billion! *U.S. News and World*

Report states that it costs an estimated extra twenty million to build a tanker with a double hull ("Disturbing Numbers" 14). Exxon could easily replace their entire fleet with just one year's profits!

Now, Alyeska is saying they can safely take oil from ANWR. They have learned their lesson. They promise the environment won't be harmed. If we believe them, we are ignorant fools. They have shown by their premeditated lack of preparation, carelessness, and complacency that the only safety they care about is the safety of their billion dollar profits.

Wildlife

The Arctic National Wildlife Refuge is rich in wildlife. For tens of thousands of years, it has been a pristine environment untouched by human development. It is an ecosystem so biologically diverse that it is unequaled anywhere else in the world. It is home to polar bears, grizzlies, wolves, eagles, muskoxen, and wolverines. It is also host to millions of migratory birds. It is the only calving grounds for the Porcupine caribou herd. The center of all wildlife activity in ANWR is the coastal plain (Speer 42).

This coastal plain is precisely what the oil companies want. Speer state, "At present, the 125-mile long coastal plain is the only stretch of the 1,100-mile arctic Alaskan coastline that remains off limits to oil and gas development" (42). Yet, the oil industry isn't happy with 1,100 miles. They want the last 125 miles. They are parasites stripping the land of all its life and beauty.

Proponents of oil drilling, such as Alaskan Governor Tony Knowles, want us to believe that the wildlife will actually flourish if drilling is allowed. Knowles points out that the numbers of the Central Arctic Caribou herd have tripled around Prudhoe Bay, since oil production began there twenty years ago. What he doesn't tell us is why. The reason the herd has grown is because all their natural predators have been greatly reduced or eliminated from the area.

Most Americans will never visit ANWR. It doesn't mean it shouldn't be protected. Some things are worth protecting just for the fact that they exist. Our wilderness areas and our wildlife are irreplaceable. ANWR, with its fragile ecosystem, is priceless.

Conclusion

It has been proven that the oil industry has a long history of breaking laws and breaking promises. We cannot conceivably let them drill for oil in ANWR. Damage to the refuge is inevitable. Safe oil development in the Arctic is impossible.

We have a moral responsibility to future generations to protect this planet. We must stand up and fight a system that rapes the land for nothing more than greed. By preserving ANWR, we aren't just protecting the homes of wildlife in a remote wilderness; we are protecting our home. The Arctic National Wildlife Refuge must remain as it is, the "enchanting jewel" of North America.

Works Cited

The Arctic National Wildlife Refuge: Its People, Wildlife Resources, and Oil and Gas Potential," *Arctic Slope Regional Corporation* (June 1995): Internet. http://www.lib.uconn.edu/Arctic Circle/ANWR/anwrres intro2.html

Dane, Abe. "America's Oil Tanker Mess," *Popular Mechanics* (November 1989): 51-54.

Davidson, Art. *In The Wake of the Exxon Valdez.* San Francisco: Sierra Club Books, 1990.

"Disturbing Numbers," *U.S. News and World Report*(May 15, 1989): 14.

"Exxon Annual Report—Letter to Shareholders," Internet. http://www.exxon.com/shareholder_info/annual_letter.html.

Knowles, Governor Tony. "Minimizing Environmental Impact," Internet. http://www.alaskan.com/anwr/knowles_impact.html

Lewis, Thomas. "Tragedy in Alaska," *National Wildlife* (June/July 1989): 4-9.

Speer, Lisa. "Law, Oil Development and the Arctic national Wildlife Refuge," *Environment* (May 1989): 42-43.

Steiner, Rick. "Probing and Oil Stained Legacy," *National Wildlife* (April/May 1993): 5-11.

Willey, Dr. W. R. Zach. "Exxon Valdez: Another Environmental Debt to Energy," Internet. http://www.edf.org/pubs/EDF_Letter/1989/Aug/n-energy.html

-Indiana University, Fort Wayne
S. Bergman, Instructor

The Ebonics Issue: It's Easier to Understand When it's in Black and White

Tobias C. Sherwood
(Morongo Valley, California)

Does your son fail to conjugate the verb "to be"? Does your daughter drop the final consonant from her words? Do your grandchildren score low on standardized tests because they don't understand what they're reading? If so, then I have the final solution for you. Finally, there is a program designed to help kids in the Oakland area read, write, and speak better standard English. It's called—Hooked on Ebonics—and it's great! Through a revolutionary new process, your child's teacher will easily be able to help your child build that bridge between "black" and "white" English, in order to keep your child on pace with the rest of the kids in California. Seven-year-old LaTerra McDaniels exclaims, "Hooked on Ebonics worked for me!" And it will work for your kids too! For more information, just call 1-800-EBONICS.

If life was this easy, an in-depth analysis of the controversy surrounding the Oakland, California school board's recent resolution declaring Black English, or Ebonics, a second language would not be necessary. But life is difficult; and full of controversy. The fact is that Oakland's Ebonics program cannot be pawned off in a cheap commercial, for the educations and cultural values of Oakland's children are at stake. But before delving into the problem surrounding Oakland's decision, and the solution to its problems, we must first summarize the Oakland resolution and its implications.

The Infamous Resolution: The Mother of Misconception

On December 18, 1996, the Oakland, California, school board unanimously approved an unprecedented resolution declaring Black English a legitimate language. Combining the words ebony and phones, their "language" has been named *Ebonics*. The reaction to the resolution has been mixed, but very strong. Though opinions of the resolution are sometimes extremely different, there is one thing that the varying sides have in common: most people's opinions are driven by a misconception of what the Ebonics program in Oakland is really all about. Most people, including many in the media, have not researched the Ebonics issue thoroughly and therefore think that Ebonics is going to be taught in the classrooms. They believe that the purpose of introducing Ebonics is to teach black students in a language they understand, or to validate black heritage through teaching in an African language. These beliefs are falsehoods. The purpose of introducing Ebonics is not to teach Black English to students, but to introduce the dialect to teachers who may be unfamiliar with Black English. The school board plans to place its teachers in special training programs that will help them become more familiar with Black English language patterns ("Should Black English" 12). This will help in teaching black students standard English by building a bridge between the two languages.

A perfect example of how this bridge was published in a recent issue of *Newsweek*:

> *In her brightly decorated classroom at Parker Elementary School in Oakland, Calif., Cleo Shavies reads her second graders a book called "Flossie the Fox." The student body here is 90 percent African American. Two years ago, Shavies enrolled in a state Standard English Proficiency (SEP) training program to sensitize teachers to students who spoke Black English. In a classroom decked with posters of black achievement, she applies these techniques to "Flossie and the Fox." Flossie is an African-American girl who speaks in...Ebonics. The fox speaks standard English. Shavies might pull words from the text, pointing out the differences in syntax. "I be Flossie Finley," Flossie says. Or "How do a fox look?" Shavies will ask, "Is this written in Ebonics or standard English?" The technique is called "contrastive analysis," and Shavies is impressed by its results (Joseph 78).*

Through this "contrastive analysis," the goal of educators is to help young black children who speak Ebonics learn the syntax and grammar of standard English, so that they may have an equal opportunity in America's workforce. Black children need this help because black children have traditionally scored much lower on standardized tests and have traditionally accumulated lower grade point averages than white children. Also, dropout rates are much higher among black students than among students of non-African descent, especially in Oakland. The average grade point average of black students in Oakland is 0.6 points lower than the district average, and nearly two-thirds of all students who repeat the same grade in Oakland schools are black ("Should Black English" 12). Some linguists attribute this to the fact that black children speak a different language than the language the tests are administered in: Ebonics. Consequently, in hopes of receiving more money to further assist black children's transition to standard English, the Oakland school board took it upon themselves to find an answer for the problem. Thus, the above described resolution.

The uproar over the board's resolution that has been heard throughout the United States has spurred many thought-provoking conversations about culture, race, and ethnicity. However, this is not the first time that the issue of Black English has been addressed; it is just the most recognized time. Books and studies in the last three decades have addressed the issue of Black English and its place in educational systems. Most of the studies had conclusive evidence that something must be done to aid black students because blacks have traditionally performed poorly in the realm of academics. Some of these studies suggested implementing programs like Oakland's resolution, but none of the resulting programs ever raised such an uproar. There have been programs dealing with Black English in many schools for many years, but most kept a low profile. These books, studies, and programs served as the causes for the current uproar over Black English.

Let us explore these causes, as well as the origins of the current Ebonics program in Oakland and the controversy surrounding it.

It's Simple Arithmetic: Ebony + Phonic = Ebonics

Perceptions of Black English have changed dramatically over the years, so exploring the foundation of today's issue may shed some light on all of the rhetoric. An article from the March 1994, issue of the *Journal of Teacher Education* reported:

> *The first studies of Black English in the early sixties gave rise to the Language Deficit Theory. The authors of this theory believed that because children from lower socioeconomic backgrounds lacked verbal stimulation in their homes, they were not afforded the linguistic resources necessary to language success. By the mid- to late-sixties, linguists began demonstrating that speakers of Black English use a legitimate, rule-governed, and fully developed dialect, thus virtually refuting the Deficit Theory. In what has become the prevailing view of linguists and educators, researchers in the seventies found Black English speakers highly competent language users when speaking in their vernacular and in some degree of control over the situations in which they find themselves (Bond 113).*

These early studies embedded Black English in our society as an issue, though still a rather infrequently discussed one. They also led to further studies which spurred individuals to take steps in the direction of helping black children become more proficient in standard English.

76

One individual who had one of the most influential early outlooks on the issue was the linguist Robert L. Williams. In 1975, Williams coined the term *Ebonics* in his book *Ebonics:The True Language of Black Folks.* Williams and his fellow ebonologists traced the origins of Ebonics to West African speech patterns (Heilbrunn 17). In a way, these findings helped vindicate Oakland's findings in their resolution that Black English is indeed a distinct dialect. Williams led the way for many future studies and articles about Ebonics.

A special June 1979 issue of the *Journal of Black Studies* was devoted to "Ebonics (Black English): Implications for Education." In one article of the journal, "Ebonics: A Legitimate System of Oral Communication," author Jean Wofford explained that "black children continue to be subjected to teachers who label the Ebonics system as bad, substandard, incorrect, impoverished, deprived, and nonlanguage," Wofford goes as far as to say that the ability of black children to use both languages "suggests that their total linguistic resources are greater than that of monolingual white children" (quoted in Heilbrunn 18).

That same year, the Ebonics issue made its way to the judiciary system for the first time. In Ann Arbor, Michigan, a group of black parents sued their children's school district, claiming their children had a right to be educated in Ebonics (Heilbrunn 18). In *Martin Muter King Jr. Elementary School v. Ann Arbor School District Board,* U. S. District Court Judge Charles W. Joiner relied on testimony of Creole origins of Black English to rule in favor of the parents. As part of the decision, Ann Arbor was ordered to establish special language programs for black students (Heilbrunn 18). This case proved to the the the catalyst for the birth of many comparable language programs in other densely black-populated areas.

But the controversy surrounding the Ebonics issue did not really take off until almost a decade later, when black parents saw new waves of immigrants receiving federal funds for bilingual language education. "Black parents feel that the schools validate the language of the Cuban, Puerto Rican, and Mexican students," said Gwendolyn Cooke, Director of Urban Services at the National association of Secondary School Principals, in the December 23, 1996, *Chicago Tribune.* She went on to say, "They wonder: Why can't schools apply the same teaching methods to the black child? (quoted in Heilbrunn 18).

As so often is the case, California became the testing ground for Ebonics programs. Seeking to address the problem of San Diego black students' chronically poor academic performance, Thomas Payzant, then superintendent of schools in San Diego, turned to Agin Shaheed, an instructor at the Timbuktu Learning Academy at San Diego's Fulton Elementary School, one of Payzant's original pilot schools for Ebonics. Shaheed says that their Ebonics program has become institutionalized in its eight years of existence: "We're right on the cutting edge, which has been to introduce to schools the idea that African-American students do come with a home culture orientation to a majority culture, European American. The Ebonics is that there is a West African dialect that causes them to speak in a way that makes English almost a second language." The goal of the program is to increase the "self-validation" of black students (quoted in Heilbrunn 18).

However, there is no evidence that Ebonics has improved the English of black students. The effects of the program on standardized test scores have been inconclusive, but Shaheed said that grades are up (Heilbrunn 18). But because schools have different grading criteria, this improvement must be questioned.

Oakland's school board took all of these developments into account and realized that past programs were not working as well as desired, so they came up with their resolution. In hopes of better educating their underachieving black student population, Oakland took a drastic, and very public, step toward improving black children's reading and language skills. Condemned around one corner, and commended around the next, American society is still feeling the waves of Oakland's epochal resolution. As linguists, teachers, parents, and the general public continue to consider, twist, and analyze the implications of Oakland's decision, only time will provide the answers to the ever-growing challenge of educating black children. But in the meantime, let me express my feelings on the issue, and what should be done about it.

Hooked on Ebonics Doesn't Work For Me

Though the historical influences leading to Oakland's resolution are indeed compelling, I contend that Ebonics is not a "second language," and should not be treated as one financially or culturally. Though linguists argue that Ebonics is a distinct language, common sense tells us that Ebonics is essentially English. If is wasn't, how would I be able to understand my African-American friends? I do not speak any other languages than English. Granted, some Ebonic words and the sentence structure of Ebonics may be traced to West African roots, but many of the words I use everyday are not truly English; many of them stem from Spanish, French, and German. Does that mean I speak Spanchman? Obviously not. If Ebonics were not essentially English, white and black people would not be able to communicate through words. I do not believe that Ebonics should be classified as a distinct language in society, or as a "second language" in elementary schools, though I do believe assistance should still be provided for underachieving black students.

However, all black students are not underachievers and not all black children speak what has been coined Ebonics. Also, not all children in the classrooms where Ebonics is being used are black. Even in some Oakland schools where 90 percent of the student body is black, at least 10 percent of the students are receiving English lessons where Ebonics is being used. This is at least 10 percent too much. That is like throwing 10 Japanese-speaking immigrants directly into a class of 90 English-speaking students upon their arrival. It just doesn't make sense. To further substantiate my point, I interviewed three people who are relevant to this research.

A friend of mine, Shakira Tatum, is half white and half black. She was raised in a "black" household. She spoke as a child what people now consider Ebonics. She maintains that though she spoke differently, by the fifth grade she knew the difference between how she could speak at home and with her friends, in Ebonics, and how she should speak in social situations, in standard English. She knew this without any special programs. So, is this a miracle, or a freak occurrence? No. Black children have been learning standard English without special programs for over a hundred years in the United States.

This holds true for a young Los Angeles area high school student as well. This fourteen-year-old black student says, "At school I speak as though I have sense and am trying to get a job. With my friends, I speak as though I don't want a job" (St. Bernard). This student relates speaking with "sense" with applying for a job, and without "sense" with talking with her friends. This obviously shows that she knows both Ebonics and standard English, but she does not refer to them as separate languages.

Another person who holds a strong position on this issue is my mother, Yvonne Moorman. She has been a teacher for a decade, and a bilingual (English/Spanish) teacher for four years. As a bilingual education teacher on the elementary school level, my mother has experienced much of what has been the focal point of the Ebonics issue—undereducated children. Though these students have come to her undereducated, she has brought them up to pace with grade-level standards. Twenty percent of her class is black, and she has not been "sensitized" to Ebonics language patterns, yet the black students in her class have been achieving at the same level as the whites, Hispanics, and Asians. Due to the success of her African-American students, Moorman believes that there is simply no need for a specialized program for black students. She believes the bulk of the responsibility of teaching young people proper English should lay on the shoulders of parents at home, and of competent educators at school.

Though I share the opinions of the above people, the most effective method of sustaining my stance is to examine the positions of people who support Oakland's Ebonics resolution.

...And it Shouldn't Work For You

1. Black children need Ebonics in the classroom because they do not understand standard English.

Black English is not a separate language. It is merely a different way of speaking English. The Oakland school board is falsely attributing poor academic performances to the contention that black children don't fully understand standard English. This contention is false and rashly generalized. The vast majority of black children *do* understand standard English. Black children watch television just like any other children. How many television shows are dominantly in Ebonics? None. How then can anyone claim that black children do not understand standard English? How many times have you sat down to watch a show in another language? Not very often. Likewise, black children would not watch television if they didn't understand standard English. Implementing a program to educate teachers in Ebonics would only waste time and money because black children understand standard English.

2. Using Ebonics as a bridge to standard English will help black children learn standard English better.

Translating every English lesson from standard English to Ebonics and back to standard English might help black students with their grammar and vocabulary, but it will take too long. First of all, the translating would make each lesson take twice as long. That would simply make teaching black children a longer process. We cannot keep black children in school for four or five extra years. That would be unrealistic in our day and time. And it would also keep black people behind other races by many years—a detriment to the entire race.

3. Black children cannot succeed in society without knowing standard English correctly—Ebonics will help them learn standard English.

The national language in the U. S. is English and it is taken for granted that a person must be proficient in it to be successful. The Oakland school board knows this. That is why they have proposed to use Ebonics to help give black children a chance at being successful. In doing this the Oakland school board has unwittingly created a false stereotype of the black race—that they cannot be successful without special treatment. This stereotype is wrong. There are millions of successful black members of American society who never had teachers to translate the way they spoke at home into proper English. I'm sure some of them spoke what has recently been coined as Ebonics when they were children, but they did not need special treatment to get where they are today.

> *4. Other minorities have had special programs to help them speak better English for years. Hispanic, Middle Eastern, East Asian, and even some European children have access to "English as a Second Language" programs. Why then should black children not have access to such a program?*

Hispanic, Middle Eastern, and East Asian children actually *do* speak other languages. Black children do not. Common sense tells us that black children speak English; they just speak English in their own way. My friends and I do not always speak like everyone else. We use words that mean absolutely nothing. For example, we use the word "smebbin" as an active verb which replaces the commonly used phrase "hanging out." We say "seb-m" instead of "seven" or "fo-jizz" instead of "four." We also end many of our words in the sound *eezay,* regardless of their true meaning. Would all of the examples justify putting our teachers through special training so they could better understand my friends and me and, in turn, more thoroughly teach us standard English phonics? Obviously, the answer is no.

> *5. Black children start school at a disadvantage, compared to other cultures, because they don't speak standard English and there are no ESL programs for Ebonics.*

The truth is that the vast majority of white children who have gone through school in the United Sates started out in kindergarten not knowing the correct way to speak standard English themselves. They spoke English, no doubt, but they did not speak it as well as an educated adult. The same holds true for black children. There is no difference. Regardless of whether black children spoke "Black English" prior to grade school or not, they still spoke English, and they still started out at the same level as white children. Children of both races had to go through the same process to learn proper English; common sense tell us that without a process of learning, no child's vocabulary would mature properly.

If this is true, would it not be preferential treatment of black children to specially train teachers to cater to black children's dumbfounded needs? The answer is yes. Should children from Arkansas with a southern vernacular have specially trained teachers to change the way they speak so they can be more successful in American society? The answer is no. It is absurd to think that taxpayers' money could go to educating teachers so that they could teach a black child to say "I'm going to the store" instead of "I be goin' to tha sto" or, for that matter, an Arkansan child to say "how is everyone" instead of "how y'all doin." The ways people talk in social situations has no bearing on how they talk in a professional atmosphere. By adolescence, most people, including black children, know how to speak in a professional situation—if not through the classroom, through another medium. A child being introduced to Ebonics in the fourth grade, for example has already been exposed to standard English in the classroom for four years; and in the mass media for many more.

Out With the Old, In With the New

If Oakland's plan will not work, what will work then? The answer lies in a program based on parental responsibility, which will run as a language workshop, rather than a bilingual program. The structure is basic, the funds needed are minimal, and the program itself is, pardon the pun, as simple as black and white.

What exactly is the program? The best place to begin a proposal is with the tangible aspect of it, the program itself (with explanation coming later). The program will be called the "Language Release Program," or the LRP. Parents who believe their child is struggling in their regular class because he or she speaks Ebonics, will be able to sign their kid up in the LRP. Twice a week, for an hour at a time, the signed-up children will leave their regular classes and meet in another on-campus classroom. For this hour, the instructor will read stories which compare Ebonics and standard English (like "Flossie the Fox"), lead their class in writing exercises which incorporate standard English into the children's Ebonic dialect, and direct their students in oral exercises. At the end of the hour the children will return to their regular classes. This process will continue for as many years in elementary school as needed for the individual child, within classes that are based on translation level, not grade level. The LRP will essentially function just as Oakland's plan does, but for less time a week (yet, more concentrated time), and only for children who need the program. The main goal for instructors will still be to build that bridge between Ebonics and standard English.

The teachers whose muscle will go into building this bridge will be teachers already employed by the school district, teachers who already speak and/or understand Ebonics. These teachers will be current employees of the district and will simply apply for the position, just like any other job. They will maintain their current teaching position, for the LRP will only take two hours a week. While not in their regular classes, they will be covered by fellow school faculty. The LRP will run at the same time as less important subjects—such as physical education or art—so the children enrolled in the LRP will not miss out on the ever-important "reading, writing, and arithmetic."

How will the LRP be financed? The LRP will be more efficient than Oakland's plan. Oakland demands bilingual funding because they declared Ebonics a separate language. Bilingual funding runs much higher than funding for a regular class. Where do these funds come from? The taxpayers' wallets, of course. So how will the LRP be any different? The LRP will not demand public bilingual funding or additional teachers. Teachers who are already sensitized to Ebonics will be recruited by a shared decision-making board from the pool of teachers currently employed by the given district. Teachers who get the job of instructing the LRP will be given a nominal pay raise. The raise will be considerably smaller than the amount of money that a bilingual program demands. Furthermore, because additional teachers will not need to be hired, even less money will come out of the taxpayers' wallets.

Where will this plan be implemented? The LRP will only be needed in communities with a large black population, like Oakland's inner-city, where the black student population hovers somewhere around 90 percent (Joseph 78). A city like Oakland will be suitable as the testing ground because it has served as a guinea pig in the past. And, we need to start somewhere, so why not at the center of the controversy? When proven successful, the LRP will be put into use in other major cities with large black populations, like Los Angeles or Detroit, Michigan.

Who will be eligible for the LRP? To avoid repercussions of the recent California ballot initiative, Proposition 209, which banned Affirmative Action programs in the state, the LRP will be open for any student who displays a need to build the bridge between Ebonics and standard English.

Where will the responsibility to the children lie? With past programs, the responsibility lay in the hands of the school districts, to create the program and to place children in it. Because of this, school districts have come under such fire, whether it be from people who claim their children should not be subject to the class-wide programs because the programs unwittingly placed social stereotypes on African Americans as inferior people who need special treatment *or* from people who claim the school system is not placing enough emphasis on providing special treatment for black students, who obviously need it, based on their test scores. Double-edged swords like this are partly a cause of the fire public education has come under in the past decade. But the LRP alleviates this problem. The LRP, while achieving the same end as past programs, places all responsibility on parent's shoulders. No longer will parents be able to condemn Ebonics programs because they are racially discriminatory. If they do not want their children involved in a program that they feel places their child at risk of being stereotyped, then they do not enroll their children in the LRP. If they feel that white society has placed their child in need for a language program, then they can enroll their child in the LRP. With the LRP, responsibility will lie solely on the shoulders of the parents—where it should be.

Will this program really work? By incorporating the methods already being used in Oakland classrooms, subjecting only students who need to cross the language bridge, and placing the responsibility of enrolling children on the shoulders of parents, all while reducing the current costs of such pro-grams, the LRP cannot fail. It is that simple. It is that black and white.

So What?

The Ebonics issue will undoubtedly run on for years to some, but if a program such as the LRP can help bring black children closer to equality, then let it run forever, as long as our noble end is somehow achieved. Though money and racial tension will always be at the heart of any Ebonics debate, the true goal for which all Ebonicists yearn is de facto equal opportunity: in education, the workforce, and politics. The LRP will help achieve this end. Through rhetoric, red tape, racist ignorance, rain, fog, sleet, or snow—the LRP will deliver....

> *Do not be fooled by imposters! The new and improved LRP makes your standard English virtually spotless. This language improvement program works like magic to tear down the barriers between Ebonics and standard English. Just ask Laterra McDaniels, an expert in her field: "It works great!" she says. And it will work great for you too! To order the LRP, just call the number on your screen or send a self-addressed, stamped envelope to the Oakland School Board. Come on, try the new and improved LRP, because nobody delivers better! (Sorry, no CODs accepted.)*

Works Cited

Bond, Carole L. and Robert L. Bowie. "Influencing Future Teachers' Attitudes Toward Black English: Are We Making A Difference?" *Journal of Teacher Education* 45.2 (March 1994): 112-118.

"The Ebonics Virus," *The Economist* (Jan 4, 1997): 26-27.

Heilbrunn, Jacob. "Ebonics: It's Worse Than You Think," *The New Republic* (January 20, 1997): 17-19.

Joseph, Nadine and John Leland. "Hooked on Ebonics," *Newsweek* (January 13, 1997): 78-79.

Moorman, Yvonne. Personal Interview. March 10, 1997.

St. Bernard High School students. Class discussion. February, 1997.

"Should Black English be Considered a Second Language?" *Jet* (January 27, 1997): 12-16.

Tatum, Shakira. Personal Interview. March 10, 1997.

-Loyola Marymount University
Jennifer Annick, Instructo

Ebonics: The Whole Truth
Ginger Evans
(Los Angeles, California)

Imagine being an elementary school student trapped in a classroom, and your teacher is unable to understand the point you are trying to convey. It is not that you are a non-English speaking student or that you have the inability to converse, but rather that you are a child whose English sounds a little different than standard English. (For example, "be" is used by itself as a verb, and consonants such as "th" are replaced with hard "d" sounds.) You have been immersed in this way of communication since birth and have not been taught or practiced anything different. This is a common situation for a black American elementary school student in 1997. The child's speech is known as

Ebonics (commonly referred to as Black English). It is a term that was created when ebony and phonics were combined for the title of the book *Ebonics: The Language of Black Folk*, edited by Robert L. Williams in 1975. Some have labeled it a tool that will "help in [the] teaching of black students to build a bridge to standard English" ("Should Black English" 12), thus making it possible for them to improve literacy skills and heighten achievement. However, others have deemed it a form of slang that fosters ignorance instead of intelligence.

The most recent controversy to arise about this linguistics debate occurred on December 18, 1996, when the director of the Oakland School Board issued a statement, via the news media, that the board was recognizing Ebonics as a separate language and taking it into account in teaching standard English to African-American students" (Linguistic Society of America, 1). Immediately, there were two extremes to this social issue: people in support of Ebonics, and the vehement objectors to it. The pro-side legitimately recognizes Ebonics as a dialect or language and feels it is essential to educating young black students successfully. The opposition believes that by acknowledging Ebonics, they would be advocating an unacceptable form of learning. The objectors call Ebonics "sub-standard English" and feel that there is no justifiable excuse for young African Americans to speak in this vernacular. This is where I disagree. After thorough research, I have discovered that the form of speech commonly utilized by African Americans is truly a dialect with a rich and legitimate historical foundation.

According to historical analysis, this way of communication has a 400 year history beginning with the trans-continental slave trade. Dr. Arletha Williams-Livingtston, a LMU African-American professor teaches that, in the mid-1500s Dutch, English, Portuguese, and French traders stormed West Africa. With their arrival, they inaugurated the historical period of slavery in America. Africans were stripped of their traditions, their nativism, and most importantly (at least in regards to this paper) their language. These men, women, and children were placed on large slave ships destined for America, where the birth of Black Vernacular English (BVE) was to take place. Once in the states, colonies were auctioned off for sale, and were systematically separated from tribe members and placed with new "family." Because the slaves were no longer with individuals who spoke the same language, communication was made impossible. So in order to remedy the problem, the slaves began to try and learn the English words spoken by the slave masters. Remembering that slave traders spoke to slaves in slow, monosyllabic phrases and with heavy accents, one can easily see how a dialect evolved from slavery. According to Leslie's Ebonics Page on the internet, slaves used

English words and applied African lexicon to them, thus making a system of communication all their own (Frieden).

The question at hand is "Why do many African Americans today speak with the same vernacular as the slaves did four centuries ago?" The answer is long and complicated, but if one examines the evolution of the Black American, one can see why it was possible. Education was denied to slaves, and even when learning institutions were established during the reconstruction period, many blacks did not go to school. Teachers spoke in the same dialect as the students, so they maintained that form of speech. A third reason for the maintenance of Black English is that great authors of novels, speakers, and poets utilized this very same vernacular so that their audiences could understand the message they wanted to convey. So if no one is saying the African-American speech has to change and individuals support this way of speaking by doing it themselves, there is no reason to practice or even learn standard English. As time progressed, this common form of speech did not change. It was not until the early twentieth century that Black English became "publicly" questionable.

The 1920s saw the rise of the Harlem Renaissance. Modern Negroes of this era desired self-improvement and self-empowerment. Education was demanded and highly promoted, and blacks were motivated to heighten their existence to previously unimagined levels. But the one thing that really stayed unique and part of the black "experience" was speech. Though there were many who insisted that people learn to speak standard English, others disagreed because they saw their "language" as part of their history. Also, the music and literature that was practically mass-produced in this decade—such as the jazz melodies of John Coltrane, "Cab" Calloway with his "hydee-hydee-hydee-ho," and the poetic words of Langston Hughes—was written in traditional Black Vernacular English. This was somewhat society's "wake-up call" to Black English being real and ever-so prevalent.

After the '20s, came the depression and then World War II. The concentration and focus of blacks was distracted from linguistic and educational issues and were, instead, centered on political and economic problems. Once the war ended, America moved into what I like to call the silent years, the '50s, the incubation period for the historical and radical decade of the '60s. The 1960s was a time for civil rights. This sparked a major interest in the education of black youth in America. Blacks demanded equality. According to William Labov, studies such as the linguistic studies in Harlem by the Office of Education (1965-1968) were performed during this time to explain Black Vernacular, authors such as Robert Shuy (1965), and Walt Walfram (1969), and several individuals published novels in the vernacular. The Georgetown Roundtable met in 1968 to review the issues at hand. Soon after this, printed studies and numerous opinion papers arose in the '70s (Labov 2). At about this time, the actual word *Ebonics* emerged. From here on it was debate after debate, and it is not until the 1980s that Ebonics and education were actually fused together.

"In 1981, the Reagan administration issued a ruling that declared Black English (as it was so popularly labeled in the '80s) to be a form of standard English, but was not a separate language" ("Ebonics Virus" 26). This announcement occurred after a school board in Michigan had attempted to establish a "language" program for its black students. The attempt never went into full effect, but it did act as a model for other educational evolutions to take place in the years to come. For example, Oakland was successful in the last year of the decade when it implemented Ebonics programs into its core curriculum ("Ebonics Virus" 26). After the 1981 controversy arose, numerous books and articles were written that discussed black history and its relevance to the highly debated Black Vernacular English and the Ebonics controversy. Authors argued against the stigma that this dialect was slang and an individual's incapacity to speak "good English." Other authors went against the Reagan administration by saying that Ebonics was far from being a form of English. As time elapsed, the issue seemed dormant, but with Oakland's ebonics program starting in 1989 and the Los Angeles School Board recognizing Black English in 1992, there was a strong resurgence of the issue.

Oakland educators say the problem is that many black students face the same obstacles as do numerous L. A. unified school kids: they come from a culture with different ways of living, speaking, and interacting than the ways commonly seen in the classroom. These children are unsuccessful in communicating with their teachers and the teachers are unequipped to remedy this problem. According to *Jet Magazine*, Oakland has over 28,000 African-American pupils, and seventy-one percent of them account for the number of children in special education programs ("Should Black English" 12). *Economist Magazine* reports that these students' average G.P.A. is a disturbing 1.8, keeping in mind that 2.0 is considered below average; black students make up more than half the entire Oakland school system ("Ebonics Virus" 26). Since there are significant studies to show that these kids are poorly educated, one wonders why there are so many arguments surrounding Ebonics. The school systems are at their wits' end, and they are running out of alternatives. Ebonics could be the link they need in order to find the best avenue to venture in hopes of improving the quality of education acquired by these children. The remainder of the essay will examine the two main arguments held by the opposition and explore possible solutions to this sociolinguisitic enigma that has burdened our school systems for a very long time.

The most popular counterargument to Ebonics is that it is simply bad English, or that individuals are unwilling to speak "grammatically correct" for fear that it is a white characteristic. Rachel Jones, a *Newsweek* reporter, commented that "...It's infuriating to hear that some young blacks still perceive clear speech as a Caucasian trait. Whether they know it or now, they're succumbing to a dangerous form of self-abnegation that rejects success as a 'white thing'" (12). In case someone forgot to inform this African-American reporter that "success" is and has been dominated by the "white" population, allow me to do so know. African Americans who have managed to supersede stereotypes and racial restraints and become members of the powerful dominant culture known as the WASP world are viewed as outstanding individuals. If it were ordinary for African Americans to "succeed" in these ever-so racist times, these leaders and extraordinary people would not be so special. Yes, it does seem defeating that so many young black members of this society feel that they must remain in the powerless class of minority, but is it really to be unexpected? This is why it is so crucial for school boards such as Oakland's to legitimize black speech. They are not saying that this vernacular is the correct way to articulate oneself; rather they are trying to instill a sense of pride and appreciation in these kids who do so desperately need a source of motivation.

A second demonstration of this popular argument appeared in the article "The Ebonics Virus" which appeared in *The Economist* only a few weeks after the Oakland announcement in December. The article concluded that, "To dignify ghetto slang as a primary language, is enough to make Frederick Douglass, a runaway slave who became the Prince of Orators, spin roun' in de groun' (roll over in his grave)" (26). I admit Ebonics is not a primary language; however, I must disagree and say that it is a dialect. To support this statement, I turn to the words of Henry Louis Gates, Jr., accomplished author of over 40 publications, and winner of the NAACP Image Award, and a "successful" figure in the Black community. He states in his book *The Rhetorical Tradition: Readings From Classic Times to The Present:*

> *The features of the Black dialect of English have long been studied
> c:.:.l found to be not an incorrect or slovenly form of English but a
> completely grammatical and internally consistent version of the
> language of which standard English is also a dialect (1186).*

Not only does Gates refute the opposition's argument that Ebonics is simply substandard English, but so does John R. Pickford, professor of linguistics at Stanford University and member of the Linguistics Society of America (a national association of language scholars). He protests, along with other members of the society, that "characterizations of Ebonics as 'slang,' 'lazy,' 'defective,' 'ungrammatical,' or broken English are incorrect and demeaning" ("Should Black English" 13). All in all, Leslie Frieden sums it up best on her Ebonics website page by saying, "Black English does have a long distinct history in this country and whether we call it a language or a dialect it is still governed by rules and is still the result of historical language changes."

Another major argument facing Ebonics is its place in education. The opposition simply says it does not belong. Dr. Spencer Holland, president of Project 2000 Inc. (an educational mentoring and academic program for black males in Washington D. C.) best vocalizes this argument in this statement:

> *Black children are very literate in standard English. They go to the movies and they watch television where they don't really hear much Black English. And if they couldn't understand standard English, they would not watch so much television...I don't think it is that serious of a problem, that teachers need extensive training in Black English" ("Should Black English" 13).*

Firstly, how can the miscommunication between students and teachers not be "that serious" if the test scores and statistics prove that black children are among the lowest scoring and most educationally deprived group in the United States? Secondly, is it not possible that this abundance of television these kids are watching is black sitcoms, shows with black actors, or cartoons? Each of these types of programs are easy for African-American children to identify with, and it is where they can find people "like them" speaking in a vernacular similar to their own. Also, these black children may go to movies, but what type of movies, with what type of racial/ethnic cast? Either way, these children can watch television, go to the movies, and get the gist of standard English, but the problem is in the home. Statistics show that the majority of these children utilizing Ebonics are from low socioeconomic communities. This means that standard English is not common practice where they live. A low income stereotypically is evidence of lack of higher education. So if these students are in homes with undereducated or poorly educated parents, it is very possible for them to grow up not truly knowing standard English as a means of interpersonal communication. Two hours a week at the movies and eight hours of television on a weekly basis are not going to help them. The schools are left responsible for educating these children. By having the teachers acknowledge Ebonics and understand the structure of it, they can connect with their pupils on a common level and possibly heighten their academic achievements.

The final argument against Ebonics deals with the funding for these programs if continued or implemented in education. I am the first to admit that Oakland's request for ESL funds (federal money used to maintain bilingual programs in public schools) was wrong. That money is for children who have no English-speaking skills whatsoever. This is where my proposal for the linguistics issue can be implemented. I propose that Oakland withdraw its request for ESL funding and redirect its approach towards attaining more money for the betterment of education for black children. The government does provide annual funds for specially directed programs aimed at black students of a low socioeconomic standing. And since Ebonics is mainly utilized by African Americans, Oakland can build a strong campaign toward gaining additional money. By doing this, the Oakland School Board will diminish a lot of the opposition's anger and will see an increase with compliance by fellow educators. This will reduce the controversy significantly and will make Oakland's Ebonics proposal more acceptable.

The plan initiated by the Oakland School Board may not be the best or most popular resolution, but it is a start in the right direction. At least with all the controversy surrounding this debate, attention is being focused on the most important participants in this: the children suffering from poor education. Ebonics has a 400 year history in this country and people have failed to recognize that. Since slavery, African Americans have had a common language or dialect among themselves. It fosters a sense of dignity and unification as well as individualism, not ignorance. This form of communication is a signature trademark of blacks in America, and it is clearly why it has remained strongly present in modern times. These students are in desperate need of quality education, and if Ebonics programs in Oakland can satisfy that need, who is anyone to deny them of that privilege? A resolution to this controversy is hard to create. Perhaps changing some of the logistics of the proposal will help, and I recommend giving the program significant time to see if the statistics change. Because if they don't, we will be responsible for a generation of black Americans with few options for advancement.

Works Cited

Gates, Henry Louis. *The Rhetorical Tradition: Readings From Classical Times to the Present.* Boston: Bedford Books, 1990.

"The Ebonics Virus," *Economist Magazine* (January 4, 1997): 26-28.

Jones, Rachel. "The Ebonics Virus," *Newsweek* (February 10, 1997): 12.

"Should Black English Be Considered A Second Language?" *Jet Magazine* (January 27, 1997): 12.

Labov, William. *Language in the Inner City: Studies in the Black Vernacular English.* Philadelphia: University of Pennsylvania Press, 1972.

The Linguistics Society of America. "Resolution on the Oakland 'Ebonics' Issue." Online. Internet. http://www.lsa.umich.edu/ling/jlawler/ebonics.lsa.html. January 1997.

Livingston, Arletha, Dr. Loyola Marymount University, 7900 Loyola Boulevard, Los Angeles, California, 90045. 1996.

Frieden, Leslie. "Leslie's Ebonics Page." http://members.aol.com/LKFrieden/ebonics.html. March 4, 1997.

-Loyola Marymount College
Michael McGreean, Instructor

Notes

Notes

Notes

Notes

Release Form

Date:_____

I hereby give Prentice Hall permission to include my work (title[s]):_____

_____

in a publication to be reproduced by Prentice Hall in any and all editions.

Name:_____

Address:_____

_____

Phone:_____

Social Security#:_____

Course:_____

Instructor (Full Name)_____

School:_____

School Address:_____

_____

Date of Essay:_____